Don MacCaskill
Bridget MacCaskill

Wild Endeavour

DON & BRIDGET
MacCASKILL

BLACKIE
Glasgow & London

Published by
Blackie and Son Limited
Bishopbriggs, Glasgow G64 2NZ
5 Fitzhardinge Street, London W1H 0DL

ISBN 0 216 90085 9

Printed by Thomson Litho Ltd., East Kilbride, Scotland.

Foreword

I read the manuscript of *Wild Endeavour* over a few glorious days of Easter weather in the Hebrides. I dipped into the book between periods of refreshing exploration of shore, cliff and moorland. Life was charged with the magic of the skies over the ocean and the isles, to which my reading of the book added charm and a re-awakening of interest in animals and plants. This was indeed a piece of luck for me considering that the reading might have been assigned in fits and starts to rush-hour trains, airport lounges or late night firesides. This book is kindred to the life I have been living in these few days of holiday break at times in company with buzzards, ravens and peregrines!

This work, written by Don and his wife, Bridget, is about the life and experience of Don, himself. It is written in the first person, and possesses that freshness of first-hand experience and anecdote so often lacking nowadays among natural historians in contact with wild animals in their natural habitat. The endeavours to momentarily capture true likenesses of shy and beautiful creatures are described with an uncanny ring of reality. They may be seen as answers to step-by-step challenges in field study and photography, picking off one species after another with precision in posture, action, expression and sunlight. Pervading the whole book, however, there is something deeper of which Don, himself, is conscious but barely finds words adequately to express.

The gap between man and beast, between nature and human nature, is enormous. The immortal words of Burns in his sorrow at "man's dominion" breaking "nature's social union" now have catastrophic dimensions far beyond that of the "cruel culter"; what might the Bard have written about the oiled swan! The real point for me about this book is the tremendous narrowing of this gulf between nature and human nature, in the person of Don MacCaskill.

Don is a forester by training and profession, but by inclination he is a naturalist who sees forestry set in a wider ecological context. For him, the forest possesses some of the qualities of heaven; mildness and mystical depths, known also to Jack London and Longfellow, contrast in his mind so greatly with bare blasted mountainside. How alien he feels is the metallic clang of mechanisation and the rip-rasping roar of power saws in the gentle green cushion of the forest; the muted sounds of horses, cross-cut saws and the clear woody clap of the great axes, are better tympany for the sighing forest.

Each species of bird and mammal is a different set of interrelated problems. The knowledge gained in years of field study is not in this case translated into the techniques of hunting, but close-up eyeball to eyeball photography of animals, which normally shy clear of human beings at a range of a mile! Don responds to the challenge which each species presents to his skill as a naturalist-photographer, with great resourcefulness and patience. The inner man is fuelled by an unconsumable curiosity in the world of nature which drives him on, even in the early hours of winter's days.

These chapters are life-sized portraits of bird and beast, revealing a wealth of detail; the fierce stare of the sparrowhawk, the blue eyes of the fox cubs, the mid-air ballet of the harrier in food exchange set my mind into Don MacCaskill's repertoire of observations. While in the narrative the preoccupation is often with the camera, the reader cannot help remark on the copious and detailed notes which must have been taken in each hide, often with numb fingers. The accounts of the dramas at eyrie, sett and den are unfolded with remarkable powers of observation, recording and editing.

Species of plants and animals may only survive if the habitat which they occupy can be very fully conserved. The animals described in this book to a great extent occupy the same major habitat: the Scottish Highlands. The knowledge gained through research, informed policy-making and planning, conservation, legislation and management, all combine in the efforts of Government and people alike, to perpetuate this great heritage of wild country. This is also a human habitat with man the dominant species, but we who are conservationists believe that man can so order his life as to ensure the survival of all these magnificent creatures so attractively presented by Don and Bridget MacCaskill in this book.

John Morton Boyd   Balephuil,
8 April 1975   Tiree, Argyll

Contents

Foreword by *Dr J. Morton Boyd, F.R.S.E.*   iii

Prologue   vii

Trees—A Way Of Life   1

A Summer With Eagles   12

Evenings With Badgers   25

Mornings With Grouse   38

A Fawn In The Family   48

Spring Fever   62

First Find Your Bird   73

High Hawks   81

Buzzard Business   88

Harrier Happenings   94

Awkward Owls   107

Royal Corrie   114

Birth In The Corrie   125

Fox Trails   135

Epilogue   149

Acknowledgements

In the writing of *Wild Endeavour*, we referred to many books on wildlife and conservation, but the following in particular were of use: *King Solomon's Ring*, Konrad Z. Lorenz; *The Highlands and Islands*, F. Fraser Darling and J. Morton Boyd; *The Native Pinewoods of Scotland*, H. M. Steven and A. Carlisle; *The Capercaillie in Scotland*, J. A. Harvie-Brown.

Prologue

Two men with two terriers emerged from the shelter of the forest on to the bare rock-strewn slopes of Ben Vane. It was the 10th April, the traditional day in those parts for visiting the fox dens in the area. They spoke little as they climbed, for the biting north west wind laughed at their windproofs and struck with merciless fingers at their unprotected faces. It became much worse as they got higher up the mountain, and they were glad to shelter a moment in the lee of a large boulder.

The two terriers, recalled from further up the hill, impatiently circled the boulder, noses sniffing everywhere for scent, tails wagging furiously whenever they thought they had found. They had made this excursion many times, knew exactly where they were going and what ploy lay at the end of the journey. One was a bitch, oatmeal in colour; the other a dog, a weird amalgam of many breeds, with a short, stumpy, hairless tail and a smooth, black and tan coat.

Soon the two men resumed their climb, and the terriers dashed away, keen and anxious to get to work. There were two dens to visit, and they lay a mile apart at a height of about 2,000 feet.

The first hole was reached through a tangle of house-sized boulders liberally sprinkled with rocky debris and scree. The entrance to the den was a narrow cleft in the rock. One of the men pointed silently to the overgrown entrance, and the dogs sniffed around a moment, then passed on. Obviously, no fox or other animal had used this hole for some time.

The little party resumed its climb up towards the ridge. The going, though steep, was easier now, but the wind became a howling monster and dark clouds began to gather in the western sky. A finger of rock on the faraway skyline was their target, and in order not to lose height and have to climb back up the steep slope, the men kept to a path just below the crest of the ridge.

It was surprising that anything could exist in this rocky waste, with its sparse vegetation and its bitter climate, but something did. A ptarmigan, beautifully camouflaged to blend with the lichen and mossy rocks, suddenly rose with a croak from the stony desert. Relatively tame because human beings held no menace for it in this wild place, it moved only a few yards from the men, as they trudged over the rocks. A raven swept over the ridge, black feathers awry as the wind hurled her about. She saw the men immediately, and instantly whirled around, all ungainly, to face the wind and batter her way back over the hill.

The second den was in Corrie nan Buidhe, the yellow corrie, and in forty minutes the men had reached the ridge above it. It, too, was a wild place, and it was obvious how it had come by its name. The great jumble of rocks and debris had been there a very long time, and the entire corrie had become carpeted in a yellow-green quilt of blaeberry. Relieved here and there by patches of dried-up heather, the whole area presented a rather dessicated appearance in the light of the gathering storm. Dark, forbidding walls surrounded the corrie, and their black flanks glistened with the moisture of recent rains.

The men on the ridge crept cautiously to the edge of the corrie and carefully scanned its gloomy arena. There was nothing to be seen, but a ring ouzel called from a rocky defile. Cloud from the west was thickening now into great banks of menacing cumulus. The terriers were put on leads, and the men made their way down a narrow, scree-filled gully on to the rocks below. There were holes and clefts everywhere, but the leader ignored them. It appeared that he knew exactly where the traditional den in this rocky jungle was situated.

The entrance, when at last they reached it, was a small, insignificant hole below an enormous heather-covered boulder. The average person would have passed it by without a second glance, but to the expert there were signs to be read—herbage had been fractionally flattened, and there was a slight suggestion of polishing on the smooth rock at the entrance.

Two creatures who had no doubts that this was what they had come for, were the two terriers. The oatmeal bitch was unleashed, and she entered the hole without hesitation. For two minutes there was silence, except for the eerie soughing of the wind as it swept over the corrie ridge above. Then a single sharp bark, muffled but clearly audible, filtered upwards from the depths of the den. One of the men broke his gun and loaded it. The other stiffened, and seemed to brace himself. There was silence for a moment, then another bark, and this time it came from even further down the hole.

"She's there," said the man with the gun, and at the same moment he cocked and lifted the gun to a better position in his hands.

Barks and growls now followed each other in continuous bedlam, and behind the noise of the terrier could be heard the frantic chatter of fox jaws as it fought savagely to repel the invader. The other terrier was in a frenzy of excitement and had, eventually, to be tied to a nearby branch of rowan. The more cautious and experienced bitch was the better dog for this task.

The noise receded further into the den as the battle was fought and the vixen was driven back in defence.

"She's going to bolt," said the man with the gun.

Suddenly, and without further warning, the fox streaked from a different hole, an exit hole situated somewhere behind the boulder. She turned towards the scree and made up the hill. With wildly waving brush she sought for foothold on the loose stony ground, frantically seeking a way to safety. She had covered just ten yards when the shot rang out. She staggered slightly, but made a final effort to reach cover. The second shot tossed her, a limp and crumpled heap, into a little hollow in the hillside.

The two men walked slowly towards the place. She lay, belly up and head to one side, the tawny eyes wide open. They seemed full of life, but in a minute or so began to glaze. The jaws were slightly open and the long narrow tongue lolled over the sharp white teeth. The dark velvet ears twitched a little, and the movement was repeated in the black-stockinged paws. Her belly, with its sparse covering of reddish-brown hair, had eight engorged nipples, still wet from her sucking cubs, and from one of them a small globule ran slowly down to be lost in the soft hair. Nerves rippled under the still-warm flesh, and a paw quivered again. That was the final movement.

The man with the gun said, "I hate this bloody job."

The other man knelt to wipe gently away the blood from the matted flank. Deep down in the den could be heard the gurries of the terrier bitch as she despatched the cubs.

Just then, the first stab of lightening flashed against the dark bank of cloud, and thunder followed immediately. It rolled and rumbled round the corrie walls, a fitting valediction from this wild place to one of its inmates. Then the rain fell in sheets, and it washed the blood from the flank of the dead vixen, leaving her pure and unsullied again. She lay there, unheeding.

The two men were a forest ranger and myself. We stood there, silent and ashamed. Horror, revulsion, and anger filled my mind with despair, and I cursed man's inhumanity and utter stupidity.

Trees—A Way Of Life

One early October morning, I stood on a wooden jetty beside the dark waters of a loch. A cold northerly wind ruffled the sombre water, and at the jetty a forty foot boat rocked gently, smoke from her ancient engine billowing across the tiny bay. On the pier, a small group of oilskinned men stood huddled against the wind, and I stood with them. This was the beginning of my first working day in the forest. It seemed a traumatic experience, this business of starting to earn a living at seventeen, and the world a big and lonely place.

I wondered, not for the first time, had I taken the right decision, or was I merely hastening the doomful end prophesied for me by well-meaning folk at home? A bad attack of pneumonia when a small boy, and another at sixteen which was followed by a year in hospital with rheumatic fever, had effectively put paid to plans for university and a degree in engineering. When I returned home to Kilmartin, in the heart of Dalriada, my parents wanted me to take a nice safe job in an office. A shadow of my former self, my fearful depression increased, and at last overwhelming instinct and a natural inclination to work out-of-doors drove me somewhat desperately to announce my intention of becoming a forest worker. Dismay and horror were expressed in ever-increasing volume and frequency, and as I stood shivering at the lochside I wondered if they might be right after all.

Suddenly, there was a shout from a thick-set, red-haired man in the boat, and we scrambled down the steps and into the open forward hold. The favoured few found their way to the small cockpit in the stern, where they were out of the wind, and in the warmth of the paraffin engine. Someone cast off and we reversed out from the pier and headed up the loch towards the still dim outline of the forest. The deep hold afforded some shelter, but as we got further out the wind increased. The waves got bigger, and the boat slapped them with her flat bottom. Occasionally spindrift flew over the bow and ran from our glistening oilskins. The engine note rose and fell, and blue smoke drifted sternwards over the propeller-churned water.

I stood on the fringe of the group in the hold, and shivered with the biting cold. Most of the others seemed completely oblivious of cold or spindrift, and were either smoking or talking to each other. Rounding a point, my eye was drawn to Ben Cruachan away at the head of the loch. The twin peaks had their first winter snow and appeared to probe the clearing sky. Then a shower of hail passed across their flanks and hid them from my gaze. Their distant beauty seemed to belong to a different world, one that was beyond my reach.

The eastern sky had lightened by now, and shafts of sunshine picked out detail. Trees, which before had been a dark mass, were now individuals. They stood, rank upon rank, as far as the eye could see, oddly forbidding. Spume was whipped up from the water, creating an opaque curtain through which detail was hazy, sometimes even ghostly. It was all magnificent. Not that anyone was all that interested in the marvels of nature. It was too cold, and most of the men stood with backs to the bow and looked astern across the troubled loch to the lower hills in the south. Desultory conversation was wafted back, and an occasional laugh rang out to cheer us up.

Suddenly, the engine beat altered. We swung parallel to the

2

waves, and rocked our way shorewards. A figure stood there awaiting us. The bow grated on the pebble shore, the keel rumbling as if cradled on ballbearings. A man dressed in plus-fours and wearing a deerstalker hat came aboard. Over his shoulder was a rifle, and he was catlike on his feet. Stepping delicately down from the gunwhale, he quietly said good morning and made his way sternwards. Completely at ease, he sat down, carefully cut a little tobacco, then took out a well-worn pipe which he proceeded to fill. He puffed away contentedly, and I envied him his composure.

I recognised him to be the forest ranger, and knew that his job was mainly concerned with the management of the deer in the area. I had seen deer often, but knew little about them. I wished that I dared ask him all the questions I was dying to have answered. A small silence had fallen when he came aboard, but when Big Dugie, the skipper, shouted for someone to push us off, conversation started up again. Shadows flitted across the evergreen blanket of trees as the sun dodged the wispy clouds. The forest still looked, to my untutored eyes, slightly menacing and forbidding, and once again I began to have qualms about my choice of career.

Slowly we chugged up the loch, the slaps and thuds becoming fiercer as the waves grew bigger. Then, just as resentment began to mount at the ever-increasing wettings, the boat swung in towards the shore and the dark forest. Our landing point was a small pebble beach, and she grounded quietly to a halt, rocking gently in the following waves. We climbed down on to the gritty beach, and then, marshalled by the red-headed foreman, walked in single file up a steep slope and into the trees. It was calm there and no wind followed us; quiet too, except for the call of a pigeon frightened from its roost. I was to remember this moment for a long time: the tall trees, the whispering branches, and behind, the chuckle of the wavelets on the pebbly shore.

Ten minutes climbing took us to a broad forest road and some buildings. The foreman soon had us organised into gangs, and after some consideration he told me to go with the "humping" squad. I had no idea what "humping" was, but was soon to find out.

All the timber being cut was destined for the coal mines. First, the felling gang cut down the trees, cross-cut them into lengths for

3

props, and then peeled off the bark. The "humping" squad was then responsible for carrying these slippery, resinous props to the steel chute, down which they would plunge to the loch. Once on the chute, the logs rocketed down to the water. Occasionally, one jumped the rails and was smashed to pulp on the rocky shore. Sometimes, the really heavy ones plunged so deeply into the water that they were caught on the bottom, but most of them eventually surfaced and were gathered into rafts. These were towed by boat across the loch, to be picked up by timber lorries and driven to their destination.

It was like trying to control a particularly slimy eel, carrying one of these props on one's shoulders, and mine soon began to protest. By midday they were chafed and painful, and as the afternoon wore on, the logs got heavier and heavier. It was a tired and thankful seventeen year old who scrambled aboard for the trip home.

I was not too tired to notice that the forest ranger was not on the boat. It seemed that he usually walked home through the forest, and any deer that he might have killed would be hung at the shore and collected the next day. Somehow I wished I could have been with him, to see all that he had seen that day. I realised for the first time that a forest was a living thing, a separate world, and one that I knew I must explore.

To begin with I was quite content just to work in the forest, to savour the freedom of an open air life, and to gradually regain lost health. The work was hard, but not too monotonous since the changing seasons each brought in its specific jobs.

Spring was the time when seeds were sown in the nursery and young trees that were ready for planting out were taken to the forest. Instead of timber props, the boat now carried bundles of plants, and a hard day lay ahead of bending and stretching and bending again in a smooth and regular rhythm. The target for each man was a thousand per day, and the trees were planted out in straight lines so that when the summer vegetation grew too high, each tree could be easily found.

Later in the summer, the young trees had to be relieved from the pressure of other vegetation, and weeding was the order of the day. It was at this period of the year that we suffered from the scourge

4

of the Highlands. Midges! They were at the zenith of their powers, and it was difficult to console ourselves with the thought that everything in nature has its place. There was no magic cure, then or now. We tried citronella oil and even paraffin, but nothing was of much use. Dull days were the worst, when there was little wind, and a walk through bracken was sufficient to bring them out in hordes to drink our blood. Midges buzzing in our ears and invading every opening in our clothing, sometimes became so unbearable that work had to stop.

The first frosts of autumn killed off this awful scourge, however, and with autumn came a new job. This was the time when scrub was cut to prepare the new ground for planting in the following season. For me it represented a period of splendid warm fires on cold frosty days, when giant bonfires were built to dispose of the brushwood. These fires were built in a special way, and no boy scout could fault us. Small twigs were used to start them, and were then added to again and again until eventually a very hot and glowing heart was achieved. Then bigger and more solid material was added, but always lying in the one direction so that a hollow heart to the fire would not develop. Soon great fires were burning merrily, and a glorious haven of warmth each one represented. As lunch time approached, the nearest fire was allowed to die down a little, and our syrup-tin billycans were placed around it to heat. When the water boiled, the tea was added, together with a little piece of stick to prevent a smoky taste. I still sniff the air appreciatively when there is a wood fire burning, and remember strong brews, bread and cheese, and home-baked scones.

The first snow heralded our return to the depths of the forest, to start felling. In those days, this was always done in winter, and there was no sound then of noisy power saws; only the quiet swish of well-sharpened crosscut saws, the crisp chopping of axes as they took off the branches, and the crunch of tacketty boots as they trod through the snow. On wet days, when work in the forest was impossible, the axes had to be carefully ground and sharpened. A grindstone was used, and it would be patiently turned by one of the men. A small handstone gave the final honing, and this produced a razor-sharp edge.

5

There was little mechanisation, although we did have a small tractor. One day, its enthusiastic driver forgot that it was not the pony he had been used to, and drove it into the loch for its weekly clean-up. Suddenly realising his awful mistake, he threw the tracks into reverse, striving mightily to retrieve the situation. It was of no use. The faster the tracks revolved, the faster the pebbles in the shallow water were churned into the loch, thus providing a steeper slope to the deeper water. Inexorably our tractor slid towards the edge of the shelf. Inexorably, with a dignified splash and gurgle, it disappeared for ever into the plumbless depths.

Sometimes our winter job, instead of felling trees, was to drain by hand the ground for the spring planting. A heavy thirty-six inch by eighteen inch spade, known as a rutter, was used for this job. There were right and left foot models available. In essence it meant ripping, or rutting, a track or drain eighteen inches wide, along the hill contours. This served two purposes. It provided a means by which excess water could be run off, and it also provided the slices of peat at five foot intervals, into which the young trees would be planted.

It was hard work. With a heave of wrists and shoulders, a rectangular piece of peat was lifted out and deposited. The action was smooth and regular, and the wet segments, rather like neatly cut slices of cheese, advanced steadily across the hillside. All that could be heard was the gurgle of the black peaty water which was trapped behind the spades, and the deep-drawn breaths of the men as each effort was made. When released, the water rushed madly down the drain, carrying with it any debris which had gathered. One short cut, we had, for getting a clean drain. It was to dam it until a large head of water gathered, then the blocking turf was removed and a small Niagara Falls released. This was very effective, but it was too bad if one of our mates happened to be working in that drain further down the hill.

I have written of the one unfortunate tractor that we possessed, but the work of extracting timber was then mostly done by horses and ponies. On balance, it is of course better that horses are no longer required for this kind of work. It was very hard, and some of them were badly overworked, even to the point of shortening

We were almost totally dependent on our horses for the removal of timber

Giant caterpillar tractors . . . have now taken over the backbreaking work

The crosscut saw and the axe have been replaced by the power saw

Our winter job . . . was to drain by hand the ground for the spring planting

their lives by several years. Heavy Clydesdale horses were used over flat ground, where their immense shoulder power was a great advantage. The smaller Highland garron was used on steep hillsides, where its nimble gait enabled it to cope with rough uneven tracks. Most of the men who had charge of these animals were devoted to them, putting the welfare of their charges a long way ahead of their own.

Donald was such a one. He would cheerfully have given his life for his horses, and many times went hungry so that they might be fed. He owned three, and he used to hire them out, to drag timber. He lived in a small hut in the middle of the forest, and nearby he had a small wooden stable. The stable was often tidier than the bothy! Donald was one of the old school of woodsmen, a hard worker, and an equally hard drinker. On a Friday night, whenever there was enough horse manure to fill his cart, he hitched Mary the garron, and set off for the nearest hotel. There he sold it to the proprietor for use in the garden, then set off with his winnings to the local pub.

At closing time, Donald emerged a little uncertainly, hauled himself with some difficulty on to the seat of the cart, and released the patient Mary from her long wait. Everything was alright at first, but gradually sleep overcame his sterling efforts to drive. The reins slipped from his nerveless fingers, and with a gentle toppling movement, he slid to the bottom of the cart, his legs stretching in supplication to the sky. His fate now rested in the sure feet of Mary. Unfaltering and driverless, she took him safely to the stable door, where he woke up long enough to unhitch her and follow her inside. Quite overcome by his exertions, he then fell asleep again, in her stall. She never hurt him with her sturdy hooves, even accidentally, and in the morning he was able to hitch her up again, to return to his work in the forest. He was always on time— perhaps she saw to that too.

The men whose job it was to care for the horses and ponies, were always on duty a full hour before anyone else. The stables became a hive of industry as their inmates received the daily grooming with brush and curry comb. A marvellous warmth from horsy bodies, and dust and fine hair, pervaded the air. An occasional impatient hoof stamped the straw, an ear twitched, or a head was tossed. The only sounds were the contented munching of hay and oats, the swish of curry comb and brush, a hiss of breath to keep dust from the nostrils, and an occasional word of encouragement from one of the men. A drink from a pail completed the programme, and then final preparations for the day's work were begun.

Heads were tossed again as heavy collars were placed in position, and the reins loosely looped. Then these animals found their own way to the work site, the horsemen walking casually alongside. Once there, each pony was fitted with side chains, and swingle tree with drag chain. The swingle tree was made of wood, and it was into a ring on either end of it that the side chains were fitted. This arrangement kept the chains clear of the pony's body so that chafing did not occur. The most common injury that any of these horses suffered was from shoulder chafing, due either to a badly fitting collar, or to one which was too badly worn and old. If an animal was injured in this way, it was absolutely essential to rest it until the wound was healed. We were almost totally dependent on our horses for the removal of timber from the forest, and their willingness and ability to pull were of the utmost importance.

Among the horses there were many different characters. Some were willing workers, others, like their brother men, tried to get away with doing as little as possible. Some, like the heavier Clydesdales, seemed to have an instinctive knowledge of how to deal with each problem of haulage, as it arose. Easing their shoulder-power gradually forward, they achieved a steady pull that kept the load moving to the bottom of the hill. Others, usually young and skittish ponies, tossed their heads and threw themselves forward impatiently. On the rough and rutted journey down from the hill, this often meant a nasty jar to the shoulder, or strained tendons. At the end of the day there was mud right up to their bellies, and coats were wet and steamy. Often they had to be led to the nearest water, which was usually the loch, to be thoroughly washed down before returning to their stables.

Once every two weeks, or so, the smith came to tighten or replace shoes. He knew the exact size of shoe required by each animal, and arrived complete with the correct ones. Sometimes he came to the stables, but more often he made the journey into the forest to the spot where we were working. Each horse, or pony, was then led in turn to have its feet inspected. Often it was only a shoe that needed tightening, but sometimes a new one was required. While the horseman held the animal's head, the smith pared the hoof carefully and fitted the new shoe. No acrid smell from burning hoof on this occasion, but a cold shoeing. It was not as effective or long-lasting as if it had been done in the smithy, but the smithy was twenty miles away and this did save a long journey and prevent waste of working time. After the shoeing, each animal was turned loose for a welcome break. To complete his work, the smith turned his attention to chains and swingle trees. These often needed an operation to remove the baling wire fitted by some ingenious horse-man as a temporary measure.

Our horses and ponies fitted well into the forest world, perfectly natural creatures to find working in the silent majesty of the woods. Present day pressures, with the need for the greatest possible output in the shortest possible time, have meant the introduction of up-to-date methods using machinery that is impersonal, ugly, and alien to this quiet world of trees. Many forest workers will not regret the change. Much of the back-breaking work has gone, but so, too, have the men who took great pride in skilful use of axe and saw. Gone are the times when great interest was shown in the trees that were grown. During the long winter evenings, amidst a cloud of tobacco smoke, the talk would be almost entirely of trees, and it is due to dedicated men like these that we have some of the marvellous forests of today. When the time came for retirement, these men often asked for less exacting jobs, so that they might still have some part in caring for a forest.

The crosscut saw and the axe have been replaced by the power saw, its armour-clad operator looking like some knight of old going into battle. Yellow helmet, with visor and ear muffs, protect his head, anti-vibration gloves and knee-high, steel-toed boots his hands and feet, and at his belt he will have a self-winding tape and a plastic wedge. The greatest danger he faces is not so much the flesh cutting power of the saw, but damage to hearing caused by the high frequency engine noise, and nerve damage to his hands caused by the consequent vibration in the handle of the saw.

Giant caterpillar tractors, with wide tracks to prevent bogging in soft peat, have now taken over the back-breaking work of draining the ground and preparing it for the following season's planting. The task of extracting the timber from the forest has now been assigned to the machine. Gone are the days of "humping" to steel chutes. Now, steel cables snake up the hillsides, and the logs come down suspended from a moving carriage carried on the main cable. The operators, dressed in their armour, communicate with each other by radio, disembodied voices, in terse monosyllables: "haul in", "haul back", "stop".

When I first started to work in the forest, we were paid by results, and today's hourly rates are fast approaching our weekly earnings then. Nevertheless, we managed to lead a reasonably happy life, and in the short term it was a satisfying enough way of life for me. My health greatly improved, and I learnt something of trees. But eventually I became very restless. The work was so physically demanding, and leisure time so infrequent, that I was unable to pursue my interest in natural history. Indeed, it soon became obvious that if I wanted to make a career in forestry, I would have to gain some proper qualifications. So, I sat the entrance examination for a Forester Training School, and being successful, found myself there together with twenty other youngsters.

Set in the midst of a wonderful wooded area, with a magnificent avenue of sequoias leading to the house, it was the ideal spot in which to learn to be a professional forester. Here I learnt the sad story of the disappearance of Scotland's native forest, the Old Caledonian Forest, and how, way back in the eighteenth century, Highland lairds began to realise the devastation that was advancing inexorably over the land, as trees and yet more trees were felled. Even they did not understand what damage would be done by the introduction of sheep and the over-conservation of red deer in the interests of Victorian sport. It was not until after the First World War, when a great demand for timber put the final blows to the forests of Britain, that anything very effective was done.

Natural regeneration of trees is nature's way of replenishing forests, and where there is virgin forest, this is perfectly successful.

It is, however, a chancy business, and nowadays artificial methods are used. The most obvious advantage is that the forest can be planned to include different species, coniferous and deciduous, to produce many different sizes, shapes and colours, and all to appeal to the aesthetic sense of the beholder. Commercial and economic interests have to be considered, but these need not preclude a forest of great beauty and interest.

As a keen young naturalist, I found it fascinating to learn how the growth of a young forest gradually achieved a return of much of the wildlife that used to be indigenous to it. Trees, at their different stages, provide homes, cover and food. As the forest grows, different birds and animals find their proper niches, and each species has its own boundaries and needs, but is interdependent each upon the other. The forest is an ever-changing world, never static, and never with the same species in residence for long periods.

I learnt, too, how in a ghastly hour or two, this precious world can be destroyed. Drying east winds in spring can bring death and disaster to the forest. The old grass from the previous year, particularly the purple molinia, dries out rapidly and becomes a serious fire risk. A molinia fire, with a dry wind behind it, can travel faster than a man can run, for burning pieces fly ahead to start new fires. It brings death to everything in its path, from small soil organisms to giant trees. It is the ultimate terror to all birds and animals within the forest, who flee before the heat and overpowering smoke, and finally roast alive encircled by the flames. One day, in the future, I was to watch a roe doe desperately trying to reach her young twins. They were trapped in a blazing inferno, and eventually their frantic mother leapt through the wall of flame. But only to die with them.

I finally left the forest school, equipped with a knowledge of forestry techniques, my precious parchment in my pocket, and a great deal of enthusiasm. My first appointment was as a supervisor in a large forest in the West Highlands, and it was shortly after I arrived there that a friend of mine, who was a keen photographer, asked me to try and find a suitable eagle's eyrie for him. His request was to inspire another great interest in my life.

11

A Summer With Eagles

Completely ignorant of the ways of the photographer at this time, I had no idea what kind of situation my friend, Mark Gillies, was looking for. The forest in which I found myself working, had its traditional eyries out on the mountainsides, but each pair of eagles will probably have three eyries, and a different one, normally, is used each year. It would be a matter of watching closely for the birds, then keeping a careful eye on their movements.

In early March I saw a pair quartering the area, and when I spotted the cock perched on a lookout point above one of the eyries, busy tearing prey, I was sure that the pair was going to use one that was reasonably accessible. This nest was tucked into a triangular alcove below an overhang, and faced north. It was, as I was soon to learn, not a good site for photography because it lost the sun very early in the day.

Snow fell well into March that year and I could not visit the eyrie until early April. But, on a marvellous spring day, with a deep blue sky and a few wispy flutters of cloud twisting and turning in the upper air, I started the long and tedious climb out to the rock. It was bitterly cold, in spite of the sun, and higher up there was snow everywhere. It was being whisked off the ridges and whirl-pooled down the steep faces, and in the corrie the deep snow was exhausting underfoot. I could hardly believe that any bird would be so daft as to nest in conditions like these.

Eagles do not normally nest high out on mountains, but more in the middle areas, and this pair was no exception. I slowly approached up the corrie, and through my binoculars could see that the massive pile of sticks on the eyrie had grown even larger. Eagles, like some other birds of prey, seem to delight in carrying in tokens of greenery to decorate their nests, and over the edge of this one hung a green bough of rowan. It was safe to assume, therefore, that it was occupied, and not wishing to frighten the hen, I started whistling and singing long before I reached the bottom of the rock. A particularly fierce gust above brought down a curtain of snow, and through it I saw her sail elegantly away across the valley. She turned her head as she passed me, and the sun brightened the gold of her crown. I watched her as she wafted herself over the glen, wings completely still, to land on a rocky outcrop. Satisfied, and not wishing to keep her off the nest too long because of the danger of chilled eggs, I turned back down the slope.

That evening I phoned Mark and told him the news. We agreed that nothing should be done until the young, whether one or two, were at least ten days old. Eagles are notoriously shy birds, and will desert eggs or young if too much disturbed. We decided that no attempt should be made until the first week in May. In the meantime I would make sure, as far as possible, that nobody worried her. Mark was slightly disappointed when he heard that the eyrie faced north, and he explained that he wanted to shoot in colour. In those days this type of film was very slow, and good light was essential.

I kept strictly away from the eyrie until one glorious day in early May. Over the weeks I had collected material for a hide, and I tied the wooden supports of it in a bundle and slung it through the straps of my rucksack. The covering cloth would be the last thing fitted and would be taken on a later trip. Photography of eagles demands extreme care, and all hide building must be done slowly over a number of visits. One of the greatest dangers facing a rare species of bird is the bird photographer who is only concerned with his own interests. He rushes up a hide close to the nest and then has to deal, not only with a shy and wary bird, but also with one that is liable to desert. No picture, however good, is worth that disaster.

I set off in early morning so that when the hen bird was put off the eyrie the sun would still be partially on it, and this would help to keep the chicks warm. Climbing out through the trees was a marvellous experience. Spring had really come, and the woods resounded with bird song. A roe buck, already well through his seasonal coat change, grazed quietly in a windblow. He was an old animal, with a thick neck and a full six point head almost clean of velvet. A few strips still hung over his face, and he was trying, unsuccessfully, to rub them off. First he furiously pawed the ground at the foot of a small spruce, then he brought his head up sharply, brushing his antlers through the prickly needles. Unsuccessful in clearing the annoying strips, he shook his head in rage, and through my glasses I could see the flies dispersing in a black cloud. No doubt some of the velvet was still reasonably fresh, and the flies were taking advantage of it.

I stood quietly and watched the buck for ten minutes or so, then, time getting on, I whistled softly. Immediately, his head came up and his ears were thrust in my direction. As soon as I moved, he spotted me, then bounded off into the darkness of the trees. Uttering a series of staccato barks as he circled to get my wind, I could hear him for quite some time as he moved away. He was probably the master buck of that particular territory, and I made a note to tell the forest ranger not to shoot him.

It took another three-quarters of an hour to reach the eagle rock. The wild call of the curlew echoed from the hillsides, rising and falling as the birds moved ahead of me to the extremity of their territory, and then swung back down the hill to where they would nest later. I sat down for a breather beside a large boulder below the eyrie, and scanned the face with my binoculars. It was still in sunshine, but shadows were already throwing the overhang into relief. I would have to hurry if I was to get my task done.

As before, I whistled and sang to warn the hen of my arrival, but my position, or an eddying wind that carried the sound away, must have prevented her from hearing me. I had climbed to within fifty yards of the nest before she took off. An eagle at close sight is a huge bird. Her wing span was at least seven feet, and her enormous shadow followed her across the valley. The golden head was prominent as she moved it from side to side, but there was no movement from the upturned pinions of the broad wings. Again she flew across the valley, to land on the same rock, and apparently unconcerned by my presence, started to preen.

The eyrie was reached along a narrow grassy rake which, if wet, could be dangerous, and I thought that the only possible position for a hide was at least thirty feet away from the nest. It would have to do, and I quickly undid my bundle. I still had not looked into the eyrie, for I was slightly below its level, but after depositing my load I climbed up higher to have a look.

The nest was enormous. Built on layer upon layer of ancient material, it was some six feet deep and four feet wide. In the centre, on a cup-shaped bed of hairy woodrush, were two eaglets. They looked about one week old, and were clad in coats of soft white down. Both appeared healthy, and had bulging crops, but one was slightly larger than the other. Birds of prey lay their eggs at two, and sometimes three day intervals, but brooding commences with the laying of the first egg so that the young hatch at different intervals. This is known as asynchronous hatching. I looked carefully at the nest for any food and quickly saw that there was none. Obviously the hen had just fed them, and this would give me a little more time.

I scrambled back to the position chosen for the hide, and started to erect the framework. I decided to hammer in the corner posts only, and to build up a pile of heather within them. Then she would still be able to see through the framework and heather, and would not be disturbed, I hoped. My ten minutes was nearly up, and it was time to go.

One other duty remained, and that was to make absolutely certain that the hen eagle actually returned to her young. I ran quickly downhill until I was far from the site, stopping frequently to watch for her. She had moved from her perching rock but no doubt would be watching me from not far away. A small clump of trees gave me shelter, and I flopped down thankfully into the heather, immediately turning my binoculars on to the rock. I dared not miss her or it would mean another trip up the hill to let her see me leave the site again.

This kind of wait can take minutes or hours, but since the birds were very young I expected the eagle to return reasonably quickly. My eyes ached, strained by the binoculars, and I had just lowered them for a moment, when I saw her sweep round the end of the ridge opposite the eyrie. She flew across the face of the rock close to the eyrie, but passed over it. The partly built hide must have caught her attention, and she would not land until she was absolutely certain that it held no danger. Back she flew again, but this time she banked right in towards the nest and landed above it on the overhang. From there, although I could not see her clearly, she would be carefully studying the hide, and also making sure her family was alright.

Five minutes on the rock spur, and then she took off once more, flew straight out from her perch for fifty yards or so, then reached the eyrie in a banking turn. I saw her wings spread out as she landed, and sighed thankfully. At the end of three minutes I was certain all was well, and turned for home. The most important part of the operation had been completed. She had accepted the initial framework of the hide, and it was simply a question of gradually building the remainder during the coming week. Another two visits should be sufficient. I phoned Mark and told him that photography should be possible the following weekend.

Twice more I made the trip out to the eyrie, carrying the remainder of the material. Each time the hen bird was brooding the chicks, but I was able to see that one was much larger than the other. I wondered if food was scarce, though it seemed unlikely, for five mallard ducklings were laid out in a semicircle on the edge of the nest. For a moment I debated where they could have come from, then I noticed a small stream tumbling down the hillside to a minute rush-filled lochan. The mallard, no doubt, had her nest there, and I imagined the hen eagle sitting in the eyrie, weighing up the possibilities. But I continued to wonder if food was scarce, as is often the case when one fledgling is smaller than the other.

On my final visit before the weekend, I wrapped the covering of the hide round the supports, but left the top open still, making sure the cover would not flap in the wind and frighten the birds. Above the overhang was a prominent finger of rock, and curious about something fluttering at its base, I climbed up to inspect. The foot of the rock was littered with feathers and the skins of rabbit and hare. This rock must be the perching post of the male eagle when he prepared food for the youngsters. Sometimes he would deliver food to the eaglets himself, but more often the female would collect it from him, and then take it to the nest.

Everything was now ready for photography, and the weather looked fine and settled. Mark arrived on the Friday evening, and early next morning we set off. Each of us had a rucksack containing food and Mark's photographic equipment. It was to be a long day.

We climbed slowly in the rising heat of the morning, with few pauses for rest. On one occasion, Mark's bootlace came loose, and as he bent over to retie it, I heard a howl of anguish and an angry: "Who the hell put the cork in this flask?" The top had come off and the hot contents were running down his open-necked shirt. We reached the eyrie at half past ten, and there was no sign of either hen or cock. The eaglets were alright, although the larger one was very much bigger than its mate. Food must be scarce, as I had thought, and the elder was getting most of it. The smaller one, crop empty, cheeped plaintively whilst the elder lay comatose at the back of the eyrie.

Mark quickly fixed his camera and tripod, focussed and took a meter reading. It would be a long day for him, cooped up in a three foot by three foot hide. As soon as I had him comfortably settled I hurried away, but not before making an arrangement to relieve him at five o'clock. It was as essential for me to return for him as it had been to put him into the hide. Birds cannot count, and as long as someone comes and someone goes, they imagine that the hide is empty. To suddenly appear out of the hide in view of the birds would be criminal, and might cause desertion.

I did not see either of the eagles on my way downhill, but no doubt one at least of them was watching me. I hurried into the shelter of the trees and threw myself down, immediately taking out my binoculars to turn them uphill towards the rock and the eyrie. It was to be a long wait. The day was brilliant and the sun shone from a cobalt blue sky. Every single object was thrown into sharp relief and tiny shadows from fleecy clouds raced across the hill. Apparently the wind was strong higher up.

Eyes strained, I scanned the blue heavens for a glimpse of a homecoming bird. My mind occasionally wandered, and I had to force myself to watch. Surely one of them must come soon. I thought of the little bird and felt pity for it in its hunger, but pity is a human emotion with no place in the animal world. If it died, it would have died because food was scarce. The laws of nature are inviolate: the fittest must survive, the weakest succumb. I was just on the point of giving up and resting my eyes, when the sun caught a small object high in the sky and far beyond the eyrie. Gradually it grew bigger, and I recognised a swooping eagle. Travelling at incredible speed, wings slightly pulled back, it dived from what must have been five thousand feet. Soon I could see its legs stretched downward and slightly forward. There was something in its talons.

Arriving above the cliff at two hundred feet or so, it suddenly dropped like a stone into the shadow, and I lost it. I was sure it was making for the eyrie, and I wondered if Mark was getting a successful picture. Five minutes passed, and then the eagle emerged again. Her wings widespread, she glided effortlessly across the valley. Her task was done for the time being. She landed on a rock to preen, and I watched her pull her pinions through her beak. But she did not stay long. After a minute or two, she shook herself and flew straight back to the eyrie. Evidently she wished to feed her young again, and this was extremely fortunate for Mark, who would have another chance for photography after only a very short interval. This time she stayed fully fifteen minutes before disappearing, once more, round the shoulder of the hill. The tension was broken, I could relax at last. It had been a marvellous experience to see this bird, so calm, so unhurried in her flight, the supreme mistress of her environment.

It was now well on into the afternoon, and after another hour had passed with no sign of either bird, I climbed wearily back up the hill. An excited voice greeted me before I got near the hide. "Great stuff! What a day!" I reached the ledge and out Mark crawled, red-faced and dishevelled. The heat had been exhausting in there, he said, but it had been worth every minute.

He gave me a detailed description of the bird. It had been the hen, as I had thought. The first indication that he had had of her presence was the excited cheeping of both youngsters, who were looking upwards expectantly. They must have known she was close at hand, for the next thing he heard was the rushing of air through her pinions, as she braked in her dive, then alighted quietly on the eyrie. She glanced, fiercely yellow-eyed, at the lens of the camera, paused just a moment, then stepped forward. In her foot was the bloody carcase of a grouse, and she immediately set to to feed the larger of the chicks. The smaller one was practically trodden underfoot. Delicately she tore off small portions to feed to her child, and greedily it clamoured for more. Suddenly, as she watched it gulping the leg of the grouse, she took off. In her haste, it almost appeared as if she had fallen backwards off the edge of the eyrie. Mark thought that she may have caught a slight movement behind the camera, or perhaps the closing of the shutter had frightened her.

As I had done, Mark watched her fly across the valley and land, but without binoculars he was unable to see what she was doing. So he had been completely taken by surprise in the middle of a film change, when she flew in again. This time the younger and smaller eaglet had its chance. The remains of the grouse were fed to it, and occasionally the hen swallowed a morsel herself. Then the plaintive cheeping ceased, and only small murmurings could be heard. Soon the hen stepped rather clumsily over her youngsters, and with wings half-stretched settled on top of them. She dozed for fifteen minutes, and only muffled cheeps could be heard. Then she quietly flew away.

Mark felt that he had been reasonably successful with his photography, although the light had been rather poor for colour. With the 200 mm lens he had tried for a flight shot as she landed with her prey. I was thrilled by this account of action at the nest and how he had endeavoured to obtain a photographic record. It suddenly occurred to me that here was a hobby that could offer many hours of pleasure and excitement, while at the same time enabling me to obtain a record of certain aspects of wildlife that might as yet be little known. We talked excitedly on our way downhill and made further arrangements for another stint two weekends hence.

My curiosity, however, got the better of me, and on the following Saturday I once more climbed the slope to the eyrie. This time, though, the weather was foul. Rain and high winds had come in the middle of the week and all the burns were flooding. Mist enveloped the hills and rainwater washed down the rock faces. Where the burns poured over the lips of small waterfalls, the wind caught the water and threw it back again uphill, to fall once more as rain. I hesitated at the forest edge and considered giving up, but a slight lull tempted me out into the open.

Within the hour I once more stood below the eyrie, and the first thing that caught my eye was the body of an eaglet. It lay, bedraggled and dead, and I had half expected it. It was the smaller bird and it had either fallen out of the eyrie, or more likely, been pushed out by the stronger youngster. This does happen when food is scarce and one eaglet grows more quickly than the other. Then the peck order becomes more and more pronounced until the stronger kills the weaker. Slightly apprehensive, in case anything had happened to the other as well, I climbed up and looked into the nest. All was well, and how the eaglet had grown! No longer a feeble, white-coated youngster, it had become a well-developed, feather-clad bird. The wing feathers had darkened and the tail was also taking shape.

In spite of the rain sweeping across the rock face, it was perfectly dry beneath the overhang. I crawled into the eyrie, and despite protests and fierce gaping from the eaglet, picked it up. The feet were very big in proportion to the rest of the body, and their future strength was apparent already. The crop was full, although there was no food in the eyrie. Feathers and fur were everywhere, and grouse remains and blue hare were present. I could see no skins of lamb, though there were ewes with lambs grazing quietly below. If the parent birds did take any lambs, it would almost certainly

20

be the weak or dead ones. All predators clean up the fringe members of most species, and in so doing perform a useful function.

I wasted no more time and hurriedly clambered down to the hide. It was still intact, and doubt on this point had troubled me on my way up. Had it been blown away, the long process of erection would have had to be started all over again. It occurred to me that Mark would have to hurry if he wanted more shots, for as the young eaglet grew bigger, the parent birds would spend less and less time at the eyrie, simply landing momentarily with food, and taking off again to hunt for more. No longer would they offer delicate morsels to the young one; it was now more than able to feed itself.

Saturday came, and Mark arrived on schedule. We set off once more up the well-trodden path. The weather forecast was good, and clearances of early mist were expected. We reached the eyrie at ten o'clock. In only seven days I could see a further growth in our eaglet. There and then we christened him "Wilkie". Mark was fascinated by the enormous change in him, and we sat and talked eagles for fifteen minutes or so. Then I saw Mark safely into the hide and well settled. We arranged that I would relieve him in about six hours.

Once again I hurried down towards the forest, and in its sheltering trees made myself comfortable. The mist was rising from the tops, showing more and more blue beyond. A slight breeze kept the midges at bay, and I lazily turned the binoculars across the hillsides. My eye caught a movement at the western extremity of the face. Much lower than usual, and banking as she turned towards the eyrie, the hen bird was flying in, and even at that distance, I could see the hare in her foot. She had probably carried it a long distance and was tired, for her flying was somewhat laboured. Two dark objects suddenly spiralled from above and made for her. My immediate thought was that they were peregrine falcons, but just as the thought came, so did the deep "kronk, kronk" call of raven echo from the face to prove me wrong. The ravens had evidently been waiting to take the eagle by surprise on the last leg of her journey.

I quickly shifted the glasses just as they rolled over to attack. As she banked and jinked, they took turns to worry her, driving her lower and lower. Their cries of victory came more often, and it almost seemed that success was within their grasp. But, with a supreme effort and one beat of her wings, the eagle hoisted herself heavenwards, then dropped like a stone on to the eyrie. I wondered how she had risen so rapidly, for her laboured flying had indicated exhaustion, and it was only when I saw both ravens land below the eyrie that I guessed she had dropped her prey. The ravens had won the contest. I swept the glasses back to the overhang just in time to see the eagle come off without a glance downwards, and spiral rapidly away into the blue distance. Soon she was a speck in the sky and hard to follow.

It was nearly noon and the sun was now high and hot. Sad to say, I dozed off. A dream that I was being dive-bombed by an eagle which struck me on the shoulder, turned out to be Mark pushing his toe into me! It was six o'clock, and I had slept the afternoon away and forgotten my duties. He had stayed in the hide as long as he could, but with my non-appearance had been forced to come out on his own. He had first checked, as far as was possible, that there was no sign of either bird, and, in fact, the hen had not returned after her duel with the ravens. He told me that he had seen the battle, or at least the latter part of it. One of the ravens had actually struck the eagle after coming at her from below. Then she had dropped the hare when trying to retaliate.

We plodded wearily down, Mark announcing regretfully that this was his last visit; he had too many other commitments, and the chance of the adults being at the nest for a long enough period to get many more pictures, was too remote.

It was now my ambition to see Wilkie join his parents, as a free flying eagle, and I climbed the hill to the eyrie on three more occasions to watch progress. The first two saw him developing into a fine strong bird. The eyrie was now a flattened platform with a residue of prey, and several times I watched the silly clown trying to catch the numerous flies attracted to the putrid remains. Occasionally he fell over in his eagerness, and his expression of surprise and dismay was comical to see. Droppings whitened the cliff face below, but the nest itself was clean, because the bird always faced inwards before squirting his waste overboard.

On each occasion when I crawled into the eyrie, Wilkie fled into

Because the plantation is fenced off...other small mammals (*Weasel*)

The woodmice were still at work (*Woodmouse*)

They . . . nuzzled each other (*Badgers*)

The boar . . . completed
his meal by cleaning sticky bits off his foot (*Badgers*)

She caught him by the scruff of the neck (*Badgers*)

They challenged one another for position (*Blackcock lek*)

A dark shape on a high branch (*Male Capercaillie*)

She is a well-camouflaged bird (*Female Capercaillie*)

the furthest corner and lay on his back, talons presented. A gentle movement with the hand always disarmed him, so that I could pick him up. His dark feathers still had a dull lustre to them, but the yellow of his cere and feet was pronounced. There was, too, just a touch of gold showing through his head feathers, and his legs were in full plumage. I had not seen his parents since that memorable day with the ravens. They would be about somewhere, their next task to teach Wilkie how to fend for himself when finally he flew from the eyrie.

My third, and last, visit to the eyrie took place on a breezy, sunny day in mid-July. It was marvellous summer weather, and all was displayed in glowing technicolour. White cumulus clouds chased each other across a startling blue sky, and deep green spruce contrasted vividly with paler green of larch and hillside grass. Far below, a gleam of sunlight on water caught a white boat, like a toy, ploughing through the wavelets. It was good to be alive.

This time, I climbed right out to the lip of the cliff, so that I could see into the eyrie from a distance. It was just as well that I did. Wilkie was sitting on a small promontory between me and the hide. He was preening.

I climbed slowly down, fearful of frightening him, until I was only five yards away, but still slightly above him. This time, he turned and looked at me somewhat disdainfully, and completely without fear. He continued with his preening, and I sat down to watch. As he ran his pinions through his beak, small white feathers whirled away down the rock face. Each foot was lifted and carefully inspected, as if there might be some flaw to detect. He lifted his head, glanced once more over his shoulder in my direction, as if to say: "Watch this!", then gave himself a vigorous shake.

It was as if a pillow had exploded. A cloud of white feathers erupted like a small volcano into the air, engulfing him and almost hiding him from view until they were wafted away on the breeze. Clumsily he flapped his wings, and again the feathers flew. Another shake, another cloud, and in the midst of it all away he went, too. He was safely launched! Gaining confidence, he dropped towards the floor of the corrie. But, a thermal caught him, twisted him upwards, and keeled him over. I held my breath as he tumbled downwards, but I need not have worried. With a lazy flap of his wings, he righted himself, and drifted across the glen to the perching rock of his parents.

I saw him land, a little hesitantly, wobble a bit, then steady himself. His first flight was safely accomplished, and my task was nearly done. All that remained was to dismantle the hide and leave things as they had been. A final look at the eyrie, and I made my way down for the last time. Wilkie was still sitting on his first perching place, and I left him there.

I saw him once again some three weeks later, when I had occasion to climb to the top of the forest below the eyrie rock. Casually I glassed the rocks, not really expecting to see anything. He would probably be away by now, flying freely with his parents. On the skyline was a large boulder, and something made me look at it carefully. Surely the small dark speck on the top was moving!

After a minute or two I was sure it was a young eagle, and of course it had to be Wilkie. He stood on the rock, continually changing position to glance up into the sky. He was plainly uneasy about something, and very soon I understood why. A pair of ravens were diving at him, swooping lower and lower to chivvy him from his perch. I suspected that he had food there, brought by his parents, and the ravens were determined to get it.

Eventually, they put him off, and Wilkie spread his wings. I saw the white on his tail as he disappeared over the ridge.

Evenings With Badgers

I worked for some years in a forest near Loch Awe, where badgers were very common. The country around was undulating and rocky with a good covering of soil, and it was extensively wooded in oak, spruce and larch, with scatterings of birch, ash and rowan. Many years previously, the owners of a nearby estate had imported badgers from the North of England and from Ireland. They were to be used for baiting, but few seemed to have been killed. They increased in number considerably, and spread, particularly down the west side of the loch, in thickly wooded terrain. Here was an excellent opportunity to study these animals, and it was not too difficult to find a suitable sett.

Badgers can be studied throughout the year, since they do not hibernate. But the best time for watching them is in spring and summer when the cubs are being reared. Not all setts are used for breeding purposes, and it is necessary first to find one that is. I had a wide choice, but eventually decided to concentrate on one near the forest boundary. It was situated on a small sandy mound, and close by a fair-sized burn hurried down to the loch. The site, which sloped towards the south, was fringed by oak and birch, and an old rowan. Spread across the hillock, in line with one large hole which seemed to be the entrance to the sett, were six smaller ones. In front of them ran a continuous platform. I was to learn later that badgers are wonderfully clean animals who spring-clean their homes at least twice during the cubbing season. This platform is beaten down by their feet as they drag out the old bedding and bring in the new. No food is carried into the sett, and any bones which might be found in the old bedding are those of badgers who have died.

I started preparations in February, first choosing the most suitable tree close to the main entrance. Against this I built a stand upon which I hoped to perch. It would be out of the way of questing noses, and should enable me to observe the animals without being detected. The badgers remained undisturbed by my activities, for although they have the most incredible hearing and scenting powers, they cannot see too well. It took me quite some time to collect and carry all the necessary material up the hill, but by the beginning of March everything was ready.

I had still not actually seen a badger at the sett. Were there, in fact, badgers in residence? I became pretty certain that there were, for on various occasions during the next few weeks I put up sticks at the holes, and left soft sand at the entrances. Again and again the sticks were knocked down, and broad badger prints were evident in the sand. Whether there were cubs, however, would not be known for some time yet. Badger cubs are born below ground, and it is some six to eight weeks before the parents bring them up above.

Towards the end of March, when the days were becoming longer, I decided to spend an evening up at the sett. There was a cold wind blowing and clouds filled the western sky; perhaps it was not too promising. When I reached the site all was quiet. It was early yet, and I climbed quietly into the stand and made myself comfortable. Gradually, dusk fell and the wind dropped. Lifting my eyes towards the dark edge of the spruce plantation I saw a roe buck emerge. He stood quietly for three minutes, before leaping briskly across the burn to start feeding in a rushy patch. Occasionally he lifted a fine six point head, still in velvet, but I was to windward of him and safe from his enquiring nose. He could nearly match the badger in scenting power, but not quite.

Suddenly, the wind rose in a swift flurry, as often happens. The rowan swayed and the stand squeaked protestingly. It frightened the roe buck away, but would this alien sound disturb the badgers and cause them to remain below? I was starting to grow both restive and cold, when once again all became still. A woodcock passed above on its evening patrol. In the future I was to recognise this as the signal for emergence of the badgers. I glanced furtively at the face of my watch, and just then another face caught my eye. From the hole immediately below me a badger appeared.

The stand squeaked again as the wind eddied, and I held my breath. I saw the black button nose twitch and lift. Slowly the head moved from side to side, and protruded a little further. Silently the animal moved out on to the earth platform, and stood a moment on four legs firmly planted. It swung its head and shoulders from side to side as it scented the air. Obviously this animal was extremely dependent on its nose. Satisfied that the night air held no danger, the badger sat back on its haunches. The legs, belly and underparts were black in seeming contradiction to the silvery upper parts. The black and white striped head was as distinctive as a road sign. I decided to christen him "Long John".

Long John stuck his snout into his belly and sniffed carefully, biting occasionally. Then he lifted first one hind leg, then the other, and started to scratch vigorously. This was to become a familiar routine witnessed many times over the years. I could hear sharp black claws rasping through the stiff coat, and a look of sublime satisfaction spread over his face. He paused for a moment to catch his breath, then sliding his haunches forward, he lifted his forepaws. Using them as a comb, he covered the upper part of his chest, and then progressed carefully and slowly down his belly, until finally he had attended to the insides of his hind legs. His eyes followed the meticulous action of his paws, and it took me all my time not to laugh at his comical expression. I was reminded of monkeys doing exactly the same thing.

In spite of the animal's absorption in his task, he did not relax vigilance. Pauses in the toilet to sniff the air were frequent, and I soon realised just how wary he could be. A sudden gust of wind sprang up and I felt it cold on the back of my neck. It was now blowing directly from me towards the badger, and it took him only seconds to realise that a human was nearby. Without pausing a moment he threw himself down the tunnel, and was gone. I climbed down chilled and thoughtful, very much aware that here was an animal which had demonstrated to me extraordinary powers of scenting and hearing.

I could hardly wait for the next evening to come, and was sitting on my perch long before any emergence could possibly be expected. The wind was much stronger and was blowing from the west. This, I thought, should carry my scent away. I soon learnt that things did not so neatly fall into place. Once again the woodcock, with its quadruple croak, flew across, and I knew that the crucial moment was approaching. I was tense and uncomfortable trying to avoid making any noise, but the wind was so strong anyway, that it was questionable whether the animals would hear anything.

Time passed and still there was no sign of activity. It was getting so dark now that the hole was just a shadow against the hillside. Then I did see that odd face again, but only fleetingly. He pushed his nose out, and then rapidly withdrew. I waited on hopefully, but nothing happened and I climbed down. This kind of action puzzled me for a long time. A strong wind, no matter how favourable, seemed to inhibit emergence, and I wondered if in these conditions powers of scenting and hearing might be impaired, making the animals particularly cautious.

Back again next evening, still hopeful, and this time I had success. Long John appeared at a quarter past nine, coming out this time with little hesitation to go through his scratching routine. Not that he was careless. He continued to pause every so often, lifting his head and sniffing deeply during the operation, never off guard. He shuffled over to my tree and reached up to scratch. I had seen the deep weals on the trunk, but it had never struck me that they had been caused by the animal. As he stretched upwards I found myself looking straight into his striped face. I saw clearly his small, deeply buried, currant eyes. He was completely unaware of any alien presence, and I could both see and hear the strong black claws as,

28

like a great silver cat, he pulled them down the trunk. His body looked twice its normal length, and flakes of bark showered down on his face and body.

Suddenly he turned and ran to the entrance of the sett. I thought that he must have winded me, but this was not the case. Instead, in some uncanny fashion, he must have known that his mate was coming up. They met at the entrance, whickered a welcome and nuzzled each other. When he attempted to carry this further by biting her ear, she somewhat roughly shouldered him aside, and putting her head down the hole, purred loudly. I thought how catlike she was. I clearly heard the yelps before three eager cubs appeared. Out they tumbled, and immediately continued with a battle that had apparently been in progress on the way to the exit. I am sure that this was the first time that they had been above ground, yet so engrossed were they with their rough and tumble that they seemed to be unaware of the fact. Then it must have dawned on them, for abruptly all playing ceased and in a flash they were back down the hole. Yelps could be heard and then there was silence.

Both adults seemed oblivious of what was happening. Long John, after another attempt to entice his mate to play, ambled off along a well-worn path to the feeding grounds. She started to follow, then remembering her maternal duties, retired below. I named the sow, "Lady Joan", and her cubs, each with its distinctive markings, "Pound", "Silver" and "Pence".

Next evening I planned to try for a photograph, and during the day I spread honey on some large stones which lay near the entrance to the sett. Badgers love honey, and I hoped to entice them out by this means. I arrived at my usual time, laden with torch, camera and flash equipment. The evening was fine, the wind gentle and the sun already hurrying to bed. I could hear a radio on the other side of the loch. It was probably an early fisherman whiling away the time, and I wondered how it would affect my badgers.

My concern was quite unnecessary. At five minutes past nine exactly, the whole family appeared. Without hesitation they took over the stage, where like comic actors they swayed together, whickering and nuzzling each other. Long John discovered a stone covered with honey, and Lady Joan was not far behind. All play was forgotten in this unexpected treasure trove. Soon, the cubs realised that they might be missing something, and battle ceased for the moment. An experimental lick or two, and they fell to with obvious enjoyment. All that could be heard was the rasp of rough tongues on honey-covered stones. The boar placed a paw on his stone to keep it still, and having licked all the honey off it, completed his meal by cleaning sticky bits off his foot. Once again I was reminded of a cat. Totally absorbed, he licked fastidiously until satisfied that all had gone.

None of them was as absorbed as I had thought. I released the shutter of my camera. Immediately the peaceful scene was turned to panic. With an odd mixture of snort and bark, they all tried to get down the sett at the same moment, the poor cubs being trampled into last place down.

I felt sure that this must be the end of the evening's entertainment, but sat on, nevertheless, to savour the occasion. It was lucky that I did. Within five minutes, panic forgotten, the cubs were up once again as if nothing had happened. I now had time to examine them more closely. Miniatures of their parents, they had paler bodies and small flat tails. Afraid to be alone yet, they wandered little from the entrance to the sett. They paused occasionally to scratch, but I did not see any of them use their forepaws in the way that Long John did. Perhaps they learnt this habit when a little older.

A little later, the adults appeared again and play continued. They seemed to have forgotten the flash from my flash-gun, and in any case it probably would not have alarmed them unduly. To nocturnal animals, shooting stars and aurora displays must have been commonplace. I discovered later that flash had very little effect, and only sometimes drove them underground. Usually they appeared again very quickly.

That evening they stayed around the sett for a long time, but eventually the boar became impatient and wanted to be off. The sow stayed for another hour, but seemed anxious to join her mate. In the end she shepherded her family below, then made off after him. I climbed down, cold but elated. What a marvellous experience!

Throughout that summer I clocked up the visits and gradually pieced together something of how this animal lived. I discovered quite by accident that it was unnecessary to use a red filter on my torch, as is often recommended in books. One night, up in my tree, I shone the white light directly at the adults. They were sitting at one of the sett entrances, and I hoped it would put them below and allow me to get home early. They took no notice whatsoever and continued with their play. I tried again one night by shining the light straight into the eyes of the boar as he emerged from the sett. I was kneeling with my back to the rowan, and the animal came towards me until his nose was only inches from the light. Only then did he catch my scent and turn tail.

Another night I experimented with their scenting powers. With most animals, so long as one is above them, even with the wind blowing from you to them, one is safe. Not so with badgers. I have tried on many occasions to fool them by climbing very high in a tree, but if the wind is in the slightest degree in their favour, they somehow manage to get one's scent. I remember one night getting to within three feet of a male who was sitting scratching at a sett entrance. Conditions were perfect and he was completely oblivious of my presence. I crouched for a few minutes watching him at his toilet, then taking a minute piece of moss, tossed it down behind him. In two seconds flat, he scented it and rushed madly down the tunnel.

The slightest sound, too, would alarm badgers. The brushing of one's hand over a nylon anorak would be enough to scare them, and I always wore woollen clothing for this reason. No ordinary sound of the night troubled them, a casual glance in its direction would reassure them that all was well. But the very slightest human noise alarmed them, and they would disappear immediately. Sometimes, after they had left the area of the sett, I used to call them back by clicks of the tongue. Back they would rush, coats bristling in alarm, to hurry down below.

I went out at half past three one morning to watch them return from a night's feeding. Darkness was still intense, and the air was turgid. Much rain had fallen during the night, and it dripped from the rowan leaves, marking the soft earth at the sett entrance. Just after four I saw the boar trotting along the path, as if anxious not to

31

be caught by the approaching daylight. As he came closer, I saw that his feet and legs were caked with mud and his coat glistened with moisture. He paused only a moment to shake himself vigorously, sending spray flying everywhere, then went below. I waited awhile in the hope of seeing the rest of the family. The rain started again, but there was no sign of his mate or the cubs. They had probably returned before I had arrived.

One night, I took a friend, Bill Reid, to watch, and on the spur of the moment we decided to follow one of the cubs. During earlier discussions we had decided to catch some badgers and mark them. By using coloured plastic ear tags, recognition should be simple the following year. Silver was our choice, and when he emerged and set off down the path, we set off after him. Badger paths are very distinct and although it was dark, it was relatively easy to follow him. The wind was perfect, and keeping at a respectable distance, we trailed along behind. Any noise we made would, we hoped, be put down to ordinary evening sounds. Badgers are well used to disturbance caused by cattle and sheep, because they do a good deal of their feeding in meadows.

Silver stopped at every little patch of bracken. Creeping closer and using our torch, we could see him nosing in the bottom layer of vegetation, and hear the crunching sound made by his teeth as he ate worms, slugs and beetles. The ground beetle forms quite a large part of the badger's diet and is the reason for the purplish tinge of his droppings. He hurried from patch to patch ignoring heather and purple molinia areas, and evidently certain where food was plentiful. It was now well after half past eleven and clouds scudded across the moon. Silver's striped face was like a lantern as we followed him through the wall into the meadow. Here there were many cow pats, and he began turning them over with his nose to get at the succulent worms beneath. It was then that the thought came. We would try and catch him!

We began to close in on our unsuspecting badger. Imagine two madmen at midnight, racing over the rough and uneven hillside, and shouting the oddest instructions. Imagine a badger cub ambling along slightly ahead, as if faintly amused by the whole affair. The torch picked him out only occasionally as we stumbled after him.

32

Gradually, legs and eyes working more efficiently, we began to gain on him. Until then he had been moving uphill, but he suddenly seemed to realise that not only were we serious, but that he was heading away from the safety of the sett. His short legs were at a disadvantage when going uphill. He suddenly reversed direction, darted through my legs and made off downhill, obviously intent on reaching home and safety in the shortest possible time. He flew down the slope, legs working overtime, and we stumbled after. Bill, much younger and fleeter of foot, soon drew ahead and started to make up on the cub. There was a hole in the meadow wall. Silver made for it and vanished through, followed by a stumbling, perspiring couple of idiots.

Then the full moon came through the clouds, and the odds were once more even. We were back on level ground, and again Silver's shortness of leg began to tell. But we began to be very short of wind. The situation required desperate measures! Bill, while still running, drew off his jacket, and with a dive that would not have disgraced a full-back, threw himself and the jacket over the cub.

Poor little creature! It lay quietly in the enveloping coat and made no attempt to escape. Gently we opened the coat to look at it. Silver was indeed a male. Keeping our hands away from his strong jaws, we examined him carefully. His body was already strong and wiry, and had a strong musky odour. His coat was like wire, and when ruffled through our fingers, fell audibly back into place. Already his small black-tipped ears had scars from puppy battles, and his black, button nose was shining and damp. His head he kept low, like a puppy expecting a scolding, but although small trembles ran through his body, he showed no other signs of fear. Using pliers, we carefully placed a red plastic tag in his ear, and he seemed unworried by it. With a pat on his head and a spank on his bottom, we released him. He splashed frantically through the burn in his haste to reach home, and this was the last we saw of Silver that night.

After this success, we now wanted to mark one of the adults. To do this, we built a live-catcher cage of wood and netting. It was so designed that the baited treadle inside, when touched lightly, would close the gate and imprison the animal. We carried it uphill, and laid a honey trail from the sett to the trap. I had discovered by this time that the badger family loved all sorts of titbits. Syrup, chocolate, dried fish and meat, were all popular, but unaccountably they did not care for treacle. Honey was undoubtedly the favourite.

It was early when we arrived that evening. One point had troubled me somewhat. If we did catch an animal, how were we going to handle it? Neither of us, after experiencing Silver's impressive strength, was anxious to crawl into the cage to catch it. So, through a hollow tube we inserted a wire which ended in a noose. When the time came we would push the tube through the netting, the loop would be manoeuvred over the animal's head and pulled tight. The badger would then be drawn to the side of the cage. In theory, it appeared simplicity itself!

Gradually the sun sank away in a cloudy west, a cold wind arose and evening sounds once more took over. A family party of rabbits, who also lived in the sett, came out to play. Although badgers do prey on young rabbits, both species do live together, and many times have I seen rabbits at one hole, badgers at another, each ignoring the other. At a quarter past nine, dead on time, the first badger face appeared. It was Long John's. He went straight to a honey stone and started to lick. This was the animal that we wanted, and we hoped he would follow the trail to the cage. It was surprising that the cage itself had not drawn his attention, but he was so absorbed in polishing off the free gift, that he was in the cage, and caught, before realisation came. One touch only, with button nose on the treadle, was required, and down slid the gate on its greasy channel.

Long John spun in alarm and dashed for what had been the entrance, bouncing off the wire in the process. Hurriedly he went round the sides of the cage, but finding no means of exit, philosophically decided to clean up the honey. Until this moment, he had not noticed us, and when we approached he went frantic. We quickly pushed the wired loop through the netting, and it was like trying to snare an eel. At last his head blundered into the loop and we quickly pulled it tight. Then we tried to pull him to the side of the cage. His strength was quite incredible, and it took both of us all our power to bring him close. Held like this, we were relatively safe from his panicky struggles, and we quickly inserted a yellow tag in his ear.

The strangling loop was released, and he was then free to move about the cage. We were now able to examine him more closely. His ears, like Silver's, were torn and lumpy, and he must have weighed the best part of forty pounds. Soundlessly he paraded back and forth, and soon we took pity on the poor fellow. Like a great lumbering bear he fled to the safety of the sett, the sand spurting from his broad feet as he hit the platform. His coat was ruffled both by fear and the wind, and he looked about twice his actual size. It would be some time before either he or any others of the family emerged.

Gradually, throughout the summer, a picture was built up of this badger family. They had regular habits, and I never tired of watching them. Much time was spent in wild rough and tumbles. These were usually started by the youngsters, but Long John and Lady Joan often joined in. Immediately they came above ground, battle commenced. Silver, the largest and most aggressive by now, was the leader. Deliberately he goaded the others into action, and soon the whole family was a writhing, growling mass. The parents soon broke off the engagement, but the cubs continued to chase each other round and round, up the bank, and on to a tree trunk to play King of the Castle. Like kittens they arched their backs, flared out their coats, and sidled provocatively before pouncing.

One night when the cubs were out, the ducks from the croft below came closer than usual to the sett. Silver, bold as ever and body hairs flared in alarm, advanced to investigate. The ducks stood still, quietly quacking until he was a few yards away. Then the old drake, bill open and hissing loudly, made for him. He stood his ground a moment, every hair on end, then turned tail back to the safety of the sett.

Lady Joan continued to take a deep interest in the young ones, watching carefully that they did nothing that young badgers should not. Often she took them searching for food, and a string of badger bodies would play follow-my-leader along the path to the meadow, but more and more they were learning to fend for themselves. Lady Joan was ever alert for any danger that might threaten her offspring. One night I arrived rather late, and they were already out and playing their games. At once, she winded me and immediately set to to whisk them below ground. Pound and Pence obeyed at once, but Silver, ever the bold one, did not respond to his mother's urgent command. She caught him by the scruff of the neck and firmly dragged him down the sett.

By August, the pattern of behaviour had changed. Each member of the family now operated as an individual, going off to search for its own food and becoming very independent. Family rough and tumbles were less frequent and the adults were not so often seen.

One night, Long John's rump appeared at the entrance to the sett, and soon the rest of his body emerged. He was very busy. Clasping a mixture of soil and old bedding to his chest, he gradually worked his way backwards to the platform outside. Here he deposited the bundle, some of it rolling over the edge and into the burn below. He went straight down again to return shortly with another load. Having got rid of this lot, he ambled over to a patch of short bracken. Grasping a few stems in his mouth, he bit them off, continuing the process until he had a sizeable collection. The bundle was then pulled close to his chest while he reversed again down the sett. A spring-cleaning was in process. I saw it happen many times. Indeed I often left them small bundles of dead bracken as an offering, so that I would be able to observe them more closely.

It was around this time, too, that I saw an encounter between Long John and a dog fox. One night a large one suddenly appeared from a hole that formed one of the alternative entrances to the sett. He paused a moment, looking rather apprehensively behind him, then brush raised in the balancing position, raced off downhill and disappeared into the forest. Just behind, grumbling to himself and huffing and puffing like a grampus, the boar emerged. He took off after the fox, but of course he had nothing like the speed of his adversary, and soon gave up. He was back very shortly and sat for a few moments muttering away to himself, doubtless about the sins of foxes. Then he went below. Foxes often use badger dens to cub in, and most setts are examined by fox hunters in the season, with resulting battles between terriers and badgers. More often than not the dog comes off worst.

During September I was only able to get fleeting glimpses of the family. All the cubs were now well grown and completely independent. They had started using some of the other holes as exits, and the main entrance became unused. No doubt the cubbing area was flea ridden, and by abandoning it now they would be helping to cleanse it for future years. Long John and Lady Joan were still occupying the sett, but the only cub now in residence was Silver. His parents often left together to find food, and sometimes I did not see him at all.

It was near the end of the month that disaster befell the badgers. I had seen Long John and Lady Joan the previous day and was looking forward to a further evening with them. Long past the normal emergence time I realised that something must be wrong, and when at half past ten Long John appeared alone, I was certain. He came straight out, but instead of going through his usual scratching routine, he walked slowly and with hesitation up on to the top of the bank. There he lay down, his face between his paws. There was an uncanny look of dejection about the animal, as he watched the path to the feeding grounds. No Lady Joan appeared. He watched and waited patiently for a long time, then sadly went below. None of the animals appeared that evening, and although I visited the sett on a number of evenings afterwards, I never again saw Lady Joan. I can only assume that she had been killed, and her mate sorrowed for her.

October came and my visits became fewer. Long John and Silver were now the only badgers occupying the sett, but I looked forward to spring and another cubbing year. I hoped that the yellow and red tags would prove useful, though it must be admitted that by this time I had no difficulty in recognising either Long John or Silver.

On a wild and windy, wet November night I was returning home from a meeting. A sodden object at the side of the road caught my attention, and something about it made me stop the car and reverse. Lying in a puddle was the body of a half-grown badger, bedraggled and bleeding. In its ear were the tattered remains of a red tag.

Mornings With Grouse

The forest was quiet, but not silent. The tall pines swayed gently in the breeze with a soft rustle of needles. Rotten twigs on a mossy bed, and a residue of dead bracken crackled as I trod them underfoot. Not too far away, a vixen uttered her blood-curdling call to the night, and her mate responded briefly. I was laden with cameras, sleeping bag, warm clothing and flasks of tea, and paused frequently for breath on my way up the hill. An indignant frog hopped over my foot and into the dried-up bracken; human invaders were not expected to disturb the forest at night.

This forest was situated in the Tummel valley, and I had recently come to manage it. It is a marvellous area of magnificent wooded slopes which stretch far up on to rocky hillsides. Trees hug the shores of a chain of lochs, and on frosty mornings in autumn are a riot of russet, gold, yellow and evergreen duplicated in still waters. These woods contain the prince of birds, and he was my target this April night. I was making for the top of a three hundred foot, tree-covered knoll, where the ground was flat and littered with the droppings of birds. To the casual observer this area would be no different to many another knoll, but it was in fact the age-old traditional lekking ground

As the forest grows different birds ... find their niches (*Grouse*)

Like a wraith . . . she appeared from the wood (*Roedeer*)

It is extremely difficult to be dispassionate about roe fawns (*Roe fawn*)

Shuna was frequently to be found curled up asleep beside the fawn
(*Roe fawn and Shuna*)

It has always been my habit to
rear wild animals in the presence of . . . (*Roe and fox cub*)

Forests are fenced off from neighbouring land

In the wild this kind of accident is not uncommon (*Roe in fence*)

of a capercaillie. Here, every spring, the cock displayed to his hen, posturing and parading for her benefit.

It is not certain why this bird died out during the eighteenth century. It may have been the destruction of its ancient habitat, the Old Caledonian Forest, or it may have been its extermination by over-enthusiastic sportsmen. For half a century there were no capercaillie in Scotland, but between 1827 and 1829 an attempt was made to reintroduce this bird. It failed, probably because too few birds were imported, and the balance between males and females was wrong. Then in 1837, thirteen cocks and twenty-nine hens were brought from Sweden. This time the experiment was successful, and it is from this stock that today's birds are descended. They are now very common in certain wooded areas in Central Scotland.

As I stood on the edge of the lek, I could just see the dim outlines of the brush-covered hide. It fitted into the woodland scene and would therefore be accepted by the birds. I moved into it as quietly as possible, gently parting the brushwood screen at the door. I was sure that the caper cock would be roosting in a tree close at hand, and he must not be frightened away. Preparations were made for early morning photography, and then I made myself comfortable in a sleeping bag. It was half past twelve. The night sounds, muffled by my brushwood cover, filtered through. The wind rose and fell and the branches were whipped together. Each time the wind quietened, the rustle of woodmice could be heard; out on their nightly foraging, the only enemies they had to fear were the tawny owl or a roving fox. It was all like a lullaby, and I soon dropped off.

The soft ringing of a small alarm clock wakened me at half past two. Outside it was pitch black, and the wind had dropped. Peering through the hide opening I could see no stars, and the rays of the moon shone fitfully. It was a strange alien world, but without menace. The woodmice were still at work, and one ran busily across my legs. Gradually, my ears became attuned to the sounds outside. I tried to orientate a slow, deep "tock-tock" sound, but except that it came from above, and obviously from a tree, its echo through the forest prevented me from pinpointing it more exactly. The night sounds flooded in, soft wind and whispering branches. Through it

39

all could be heard the strange "tocks", now running together to end in a gentle sizzle. This sound could only be coming from a capercaillie cock, and although it was but three o'clock and would be hours before any photographic action was possible, it so excited me that I rechecked everything by the light of my torch.

Cups of tea and chocolate passed the time away, and for entertainment I listened to the fascinating song of the capercaillie. The sound kept coming and going, rising and falling, still impossible to pinpoint. I discovered afterwards that these variations of sound were caused by the swinging of his head from side to side, and by the changing of his position on the branch. About half past three the song became louder and more insistent. The "tocks" were repeated three or four times relatively slowly, then run together into a rapid ripple of "tocks", which ended in a soft sizzle and an explosive splutter. The final sound is best likened to an explosion of gas from a bottle.

As daylight filtered through the trees I could see him at last. He stood against the lightening eastern sky, a dark shape on a high branch, shuffling slowly up and down its slender length, his great feathered tail fanned out, and only just keeping his balance. He continued his splendid performance, an operatic tenor at the height of his powers, only pausing occasionally for breath. As dawn broke, his song achieved a greater urgency. Surely, he would soon fly down to the lek.

The dawn chorus started. Below, on the waters of the loch, oystercatchers were piping and mallard awakening. The resident greylags took to the air and their mournful cries faded into the distance. A tawny owl hooted and then was gone. Now, a pigeon cooed softly from the branch of a pine, before taking off with a rustle of wing pinions. Away in the distance I could hear the black-cock croodling, and I promised myself a visit to their lek as soon as possible. Near at hand the capercaillie cock reached a final crescendo in his song, then flew clumsily on to the lek.

In the centre of the area there was a tree stump, and he strode to it, feathers fanned. As he stood on it, with tail and neck feathers blown out, I realised just how large he was. His body, at least three feet in length, had feathers of a beautiful greenish-black sheen, and there was a brilliant red stripe above his eyes. On each shoulder was a distinctive white spot. His song rang out again: "tocks", sizzles, and splutters following quickly upon each other. I watched entranced, as the glossy green throat feathers swelled from his neck, and the great black tail with grey markings fanned out like that of a turkey. Deep down, his throat throbbed with his efforts, pulsing in unison with the sound from his horn-coloured beak. Stepping down from his moss-covered platform, he stalked proudly, like a galleon under full sail, across his domain. Every now and then he leapt six feet into the air and flew a few yards before landing clumsily. It was a magnificent performance, and it was a pity that there was insufficient light to record it on film. I fretted that he would be gone before the light came.

Rays of sunrise began to highlight the trees. A little wren sat on the protruding lens of my camera and started his ratchet song. He ceased only after I put out a cautious finger to frighten him away. As the light intensified, so did the song of the caper diminish. He was pausing now for longer periods, and looking up into the surrounding trees as if searching for something special. Gently his song died away, and soon only slow "tock-tocks" could be heard. He started to peck at the ground and I knew the lek was over.

It was half past six when, suddenly, he took off. He landed on a pine tree a few hundred yards away and began to feed. Slowly relaxing after my four hour vigil, which had passed all too quickly, I waited until he had moved further away, before packing up and crawling out. As I emerged the sun broke through properly, and into its rays flew the hen caper from a nearby tree. I caught a glimpse of a beautiful brown bird, smaller than its mate, and with a lovely rufous breast.

Later that week, around four o'clock in the morning, when frost whitened the ground and pine needles sparkled like diamonds in the light of my torch, I set off up the path to the blackcock lek. It was narrow and winding, a secret trail into the heart of the forest. Little pools of ice crackled beneath my feet and the grass was bowed down by the weight of the frost. The darkness was still intense, broken only by the cold light of millions of stars above. There was a sudden break in the tree canopy, and an open area of heather stretched away into the darkness. Bisecting the area was a dyke, on one side of which was the forest, and on the other a grass meadow. The blackcock lek was partly in the forest and partly in the field.

My hide, built the previous evening, was in the field where the grass was flattened into patches, each a square yard in extent, and each representing the territory of a cock bird. Droppings were everywhere, for the ceremony of the lek had been building up over the past three or four weeks. The birds had not yet arrived, but I hurried into the hide just in case, and set up the camera. It was a quarter past four, and pleasant to get out of the light frosty wind into comparative shelter.

Suddenly, there was a flutter of wings and a dull thud. The first bird had arrived, but it was still too dark to see more than ten yards. Soon the sound of wing beats filled the air, and with this the first vocal sounds came from the birds. At five, it was possible to see across the lek and count twenty-five males. They were separated from each other by eight to ten feet, and very soon feathers began to fly as they challenged one another for position. The battle cry between cocks, a harsh "cook-a-coorie, cook-a-coorie" rang out, and was followed by a hissing "chooii, chooii". With wings extended, and lyre-shaped tails fanned, they ran towards each other, crashing together with both feet off the ground. Like two fencers, each couple retreated, only to come together again. Strutting and parading, tails fanned and red eye-stripe aflame, the whole field soon rang out with the continuous bubbling and crooning of twenty-five blackcock. The sound was unceasing, one's ears were overwhelmed with the noise, and it was impossible, peering through first one hole then another in the covering of the hide, to follow all the action.

A cock, quite close to me, had a game leg, and was easily identified. I called him "Limpy". He hobbled towards his nearest neighbour. Wings flashed and crashed, and his opponent crowed triumphantly before they both retreated. The light improved and detail became much clearer. Frost was thick on the ground and the birds were silhouetted against its brilliance. A silence fell suddenly, and lasted perhaps ten seconds. After the hullabaloo, it was quite startling. Then one bird uttered the "cook-a-coorie" cry again, and soon they were all at it once more. There was a rush of wings, and a young male attempted to intrude from the edge of the lek. He landed in the central area and took up a stance. Three cocks rushed at him, and he was driven off, running the gauntlet of others as he fled to the outer edge again.

The central area of a lek is the elite ground, and the reason was soon to emerge. Three hens flew in and landed there. Immediately, two cocks broke off their duelling and made for them. Seemingly unconcerned, they walked around pecking the ground, pretending there was nothing unusual in the circumstances. Two were mated and the third turned towards another male, who immediately mounted her. Then all three hens separated and went their independent ways through the lek, being mated by any nearby cocks that they happened to pass. One of them arrived in front of the hide, and a duel between Limpy and a rival cock began. Limpy drove off his opponent and mated with the hen, the event lasting just five seconds before she wandered off again towards the outer edge of the lek.

Other sounds began to intrude through the croodling of the black-cocks. The wistful cry of a curlew seemed close to me as the bird awoke to another day and flew off to feed, his plaintive call rising and falling into the distance. A pipit spun up towards the rising sun, and jerkily descended again on outspread wings, singing strongly. Far away I could just hear the sharp tapping of a great spotted woodpecker and the piping of a pair of oystercatchers. Suddenly, a loud "moo" echoed over the lek, and I realised that the crofter was up and his cows, like the blackcock, were on parade. One came into view and crossed over the lek. I distinctly saw two wholly engrossed cocks doing battle beneath her belly. A light mist billowed up and around the lek, and soon only the ghostly forms of blackcock were visible.

By seven, the sun had broken through, and I began to think of photography. It became apparent that there was a blue and green tinge in the "black" of the blackcock. The tail coverts were very white, and the eyebrows, caught by the rays of the cold sun, were thick and red. They bowed to each other before advancing, and their cries soon reached a new crescendo which made my ears ring.

With so much action, it was difficult to concentrate on only one pair of birds, but now that photography was possible, it was necessary to select a couple. Limpy and his opponent seemed the obvious choice. Sometimes they wandered away from their stances, but returned when they wished to do battle. Limpy eventually broke off the engagement entirely, standing with shoulders hunched and bill depressed. His adversary, still with some energy left, turned and challenged another neighbour, and soon they, too, were joined in strife. It was obvious that the battles were not in any way serious, and except for the loss of a few feathers, none of the birds came to any harm.

As eight o'clock approached, the action diminished. Birds stood around, apparently undecided, only occasionally bursting into activity. They seemed at a loose end, not knowing quite what to do, perhaps waiting for a signal from their leader. The cows returned, and the cocks stepped slowly aside, as they grazed through the lek. By half past eight it was necessary for me to leave, and I could not wait any longer for them to make up their minds. As I stepped out of the hide, every bird woke up and took off with a rush of wings for the safety of the trees.

That spring I spent many happy nights out with capercaillie and blackcock. The caper's activity varied a good deal. Sometimes his song did not start until nearly four o'clock, when he would fly straight down to the lek, spend only two hours there, and then take off again at six. One morning I heard him fly down to the ground, but he did not appear on the lek, although he could be plainly heard going through his repetoire close by. He was about one hundred yards away displaying on another little knoll, and I wondered if he had been frightened by snores coming from my hide. Branches spread over this spot later in the day made sure that he would return to his original parade ground.

Photography of this bird was quite an arduous and chancy business. By the middle of April he was in full song, but there were occasions when for some unknown reason he did not come to the lek at all. One could never be sure, the evening before, whether the weather would be kind the next morning, and the hide had to be entered before half past two. One never quite knew when he would

44

fly off to feed, but it could well be just when the light was right. At this time of the month the sun touched his lek at about half past six, and remained on it for half an hour or so. But by half past six he had probably passed the peak of his display, and it was difficult to catch him with tail fanned and neck feathers erect. There is a limit to the number of consecutive early morning risings one can endure and be fit for work the rest of the day!

One morning, I caught the caper cock on the lek with a strange visitor. It was a brown hare, and he was hopping casually around. The caper, after a short pause in his song and a long look at the hare, continued with his parade, he keeping to his side of the lek and the hare to the other. Neither seemed at all concerned by the presence of the other. No doubt they had met there before.

The hen came to the cock on only a few occasions, though he could often be seen staring into the surrounding trees apparently looking for her. Sometimes she answered his song with her mallard-like call, and one morning she strode casually on to the lek at about six o'clock. He was already in the throes of his song, but perhaps her arrival took him by surprise, for he lost the thread of it for a moment. Quickly recovering, he was soon back in full voice, following her around and making little runs towards her.

The hen completely ignored him, walking slowly and pecking at the ground. It seemed there were more important matters for her to attend to. She kept edging towards the boundary of the lek, and he then became quite agitated, herding her back towards the centre. At times it really looked as though she regarded his rather pompous behaviour with amused indifference. For me, the climax arrived when she came close to my hide and stood for a moment staring straight at me. Behind, in all his glory, with tail completely fanned, and in full display, stood her mate, dwarfing her completely. It was a marvellous picture, and I cursed that there was not enough light for photography.

Towards the end of April I made my last visit to the lek of the capercaillie, hoping for a final photograph. By half past six he had not appeared, although I could hear him in the trees above. At a quarter to eight I packed up, and was waiting for him to fly away, when I heard him take off from his perch and alight somewhere behind the hide. From there, suddenly, came the most pig-like grunts, and never having heard this sound before, one might have been excused for thinking that a pig had materialised from nowhere. Then my caper cock paraded on to the lek, flew on to his favourite stump, and gave me his final song for the season.

There were plenty of visits to the blackcock lek, too, but here there seemed to be no irregularity of appearances or behaviour. They always turned up, and so far as I could see, each cock had his own stance. Limpy was always there, on the same spot. A master cock, he had the power to hold his position near the centre. Obviously some interchange must take place because the fringe birds fought to improve their positions. No immature male was allowed to intrude into the central arena, and was always driven off by master cocks who combined together to carry out this duty. Hen birds did not always turn up, but when they did, the sequence of events was always the same. They landed in the middle of the lek, were mated, and slowly filtered out to the edge. It is not known whether all the greyhens are mated on the lek, but it seems likely, for by this means it is ensured that fertilisation is brought about by the strongest birds.

I paid my last visit to this lek early in May. The morning was black and my torch failed to pick out the hide. Eventually I found it, a sad bundle of cloth, flattened and trampled by the curious cows.

In the middle of May I returned to the capercaillie lekking ground, and found the hen nesting on the knoll that was in the middle of the cock's territory. She is a well-camouflaged bird, not easily seen, and tends to sit tight until nearly stood upon. It nearly happened on this occasion. She rose from the root of a pine just as I was about to step on the nest. Her eight buff-coloured eggs lay in a simple scrape. This she had set on a fairly steep slope. Being a rather heavy bird, this would enable her to take off more easily.

I decided to try for a photograph, and in a day or two had erected a simple wooden frame twenty feet away. She accepted it quite happily, and when a suitable sunny weekend came, I fixed the cover and got someone to see me into the hide. One hour later she landed about two hundred yards away, and began warily to make her way to the nest. She crouched low, using branchwood for cover, and was frequently lost to sight in the undergrowth. Suddenly she was there, standing with head cocked. I "shot" her before she settled down on her eggs, shuffling and turning until she was comfortable.

The cock takes no part whatsoever in the incubation process, spending most of his time in the tree tops and leaving the hen to her lonely vigil. This cock, however, as I was to discover later, actively defended the territory in which his mate nested. After hatching, the young remain at the nest only long enough to dry off, and are then led away by the hen. I wanted a picture of them while they were still at the nest.

One day I came up to see how near they were to hatching. I was in sight of the nest when, suddenly, the cock appeared from a group of small trees. With tail feathers fanned and neck ruffled, as at lekking time, he barred my way. I tried to side-step, but each time he out-manoeuvred me and rushed at my boots, at the same time flapping his wings and making pig-like grunts. Nothing I could do would deter him, and short of forcing him aside at the risk of a severe pecking, there was no option but to turn tail. He harried me down the hill right on to the road, and I gave him best.

I gave him a few days in which to recover, then tried again. With great care I crept all the way, keeping under cover as far as possible and avoiding tell-tale twigs and branches. Triumphantly I reached the hide without receiving his attentions.

All that remained of the nest was a little pile of egg shell, and I could imagine him in a tree not far away, looking rather smug about it all.

A Fawn In The Family

The phone call came just as I was settling down one evening early in June. A friend who lived in Cowal was at the other end of the line. Could I please do something to help a young roe deer fawn which his terriers had found that morning? I sighed as I thought back to similar happenings of previous years. Without fail, and every year, someone finds a little deer which he imagines is lost. But bird and animal mothers do not mislay their young, any more than human mothers do, and most of these young animals, found and carried home, will die as a result of improper handling and feeding. Of course accidents can happen in consequence of which young animals are lost, but that kind of occurrence is the exception and not the rule.

My caller's case was different, however. He had been out in the forest that morning exercising his dogs. Running ahead of him, they had disturbed a little fawn. Normally young roe fawns are helpless for the first ten days or so of their lives, lying quiet and vulnerable where the doe has dropped them at birth, and being suckled periodically by her when she returns for that purpose. With their beautifully mottled coats they are not easily seen against the surrounding vegetation, and it is therefore by chance that a predator, such as fox or wildcat, or even dog, comes upon them.

This one was a buck. He must have been over the helpless stage because he rose and ran when the dogs came upon him. He would weigh about six pounds at this age, and to the dogs would have the appearance of a hare. Had he been even one week older, his longer legs would have left them far behind. They caught up with him quite quickly, but out of my caller's sight. By the time he reached them, they were over their first surprise and were ready to pounce. Probably the fact that the fawn was lying motionless had made them hesitate. My friend was unable to decide exactly which spot he had risen from originally, but hopefully carried him some way back along the track, deciding to return later to make sure that the mother had successfully found her offspring.

Later in the day, however, the little one was still lying in the same position with no obvious signs that the mother had been back. The fact that the fawn was still there was a good enough indication that she had either failed to find him, or had been deterred by the smell of dog. Handling by human beings will not normally discourage a doe from returning to her fawn. There was no option but to carry the youngster home. We arranged to meet at Inveraray, and within the hour I had taken charge of the little buck.

It is extremely difficult to be dispassionate about roe fawns. With their beautifully spotted coats, large violet eyes with long lashes, and endearing curved black moustaches, they are irresistible. Indeed, it is this appealing beauty, as much as their helplessness, that tempts people to try to succour them. They are one of nature's gems. I packed this one gently into a hay box, and the journey home was uneventful.

I knew that he would be weak through lack of food and that it was essential, if he was to survive, to get something into him. From past experience I also knew that this was easier said than done. Luckily I had some Ostermilk and an old feeding bottle from a previous rearing. I mixed a small quantity and presented it to him. As expected, he completely rejected it. This youngster had suckled its mother for at least ten days, and the child/parent bond was already strong. Much has been written about the imprint bond, and pioneers such as Konrad Lorenz have repeatedly shown that the first object an animal or bird sees when born, becomes its mother. Konrad Lorenz worked mainly with geese, and found that they would even reject their own kind, when adult, to follow their human parent.

This natural bond between the animal and its young is not easily broken, but I once did it quite accidentally. Driving beside a loch, I saw ahead a mallard mother crossing the road with her young brood. I drove up and waited until she had them safely across, and then jumped out to follow their progress into the ditch. Suddenly another youngster appeared and started to cross over to join them. When it came to my feet, however, it stopped and called to me. I stood still hoping that it would go away, but to no avail. I picked it up and carried it to the spot from which its brethren had vanished. Before I was back at the car the duckling was at my feet again. Twice more I carried it away and each time it was at my heels when I turned to look. I certainly did not want a duckling, but in the end I had no option but to take it home and rear it.

Having rejected my first offering, the fawn had now to be forcibly fed. This meant prising open the mouth and pouring small spoonfuls down its throat. This is always a difficult job and one feels some distaste at treating an animal in this fashion, but unless it is fed it will surely die, and one therefore has no alternative. The older they are the more they resist, and however weak and hungry cannot be persuaded to drink voluntarily.

I held him grimly as he kicked out. His incredibly strong slim legs, with their dainty black hooves still soft and pliable, were fairly easy to hold. He cried piteously, like a child, calling to his real mother for help, and of course, in the wild she would have come running at that sound. Milk dripped everywhere, messing up his silky coat and whitening his muzzle. The surplus fell on to the carpet; and this was the cause of an improvement in the situation. It has always been my habit to rear wild animals in the presence of domestic pets, for they seem to provide some reassurance to their wild brethren. My labrador, Shuna, had been sitting quietly beside me, occasionally restive at the fawn's struggles, but for the most part still, being used to these scenes. Now, she decided to clean up the mess on the floor, and from there it was a natural progression to continue the process upon the fawn's milky face. Her rough tongue seemed to reassure him, and he gradually quietened. Even so, by late evening, he had swallowed no more than two ounces. It was going to be a busy night.

By this time the fawn had acquired a name. With normal development in mind, I hopefully called him "Bounce"! I settled him as comfortably as possible in his box and laid my sleeping bag close by. Shuna curled up beside us, and during the night patiently cleaned up both the fawn and the floor. Each feed was a battle of wills, but each time a minute quantity went down his throat in spite of his protests. I tried various tactics. Sometimes I pushed his face into the bowl so that his nostrils were covered, but each time he blew furiously, thus creating a frothy milk volcano. I experimented with a finger dipped into milk and presented to him for sucking, but to no avail. The only course was to forcibly pour a little down his throat. Poor Bounce!

By morning he had taken just enough for survival, and I persevered in this fashion for the next few days. Much patience is needed, and in moments of exasperation one almost curses the silly little animal for not realising that one is trying to help it to survival. But at the end of four or five days, one is usually rewarded by a slight pressure on the finger. It has got the idea at last. It is a fairly quick transition from this point to the use of a teat, when the milk will be taken more quickly and in greater quantities. It still has to be carefully mixed to bring it as close as possible to the natural in quality and quantity. The change over from the mother's milk can often bring scour in its wake, and this, if left untreated, can further weaken the animal.

Bounce followed the usual behaviour pattern in the matter of feeding, and once he had made this step forward, there was no holding him back. The imprinted bond between the fawn and its natural mother was now broken, and I had taken her place. He grew fast and began to develop into a strong little buck. I was still sleeping with him, but the nights were anything but peaceful. Between feeds he would scramble all over me, his small black hooves digging through the sleeping bag and into my ribs. His nightly wanderings also had an unfortunate effect on my room, which soon proclaimed that complete redecoration would be necessary at the end of the operation. It had been imperative to keep him somewhere that was warm, and at that time a small general purpose room in the house had seemed the best solution. You cannot house-train a small fawn who is fighting for survival, and Bounce was no different to any other in the matter of a call of nature. He also learnt to rub his coat along one of the walls, and this soon put paid to the wallpaper. As soon as possible I built him a small pen in the garden.

So the days went by. Bounce settled down in his pen and continued to flourish. The domestic pets accepted him completely as one of the family. Shuna was frequently to be found curled up asleep beside the fawn, and her motherly concern for his toilet continued. Cleaning up operations were frequent and thorough. The cat, Cassius, a somewhat reluctant companion to a previous fawn, took this one to his heart, often sharing an afternoon siesta with it. He followed Bounce about in a devoted fashion, occasionally reaching up to rub his head on the buck's chin, or arching his back beneath his belly. The buck would "peep" plaintively when he knew a meal was due, then come running whenever he heard the garden gate click. He would swallow his milk in double quick time, race through the pellets, and then run off to nibble rose petals by way of "afters". My roses were pruned rather early that year! Cassius appointed himself guardian of the buck's rations, and when the pet rabbits endeavoured to steal a pellet or two, would firmly chase them off without harming them in any way. This relationship between the cat and the buck was not a transient thing, but lasted until Bounce was quite old.

By September his spots had faded. His habits, too, had gradually changed, and now he lay up during the day in a shady spot, chewing the cud as his wild brothers would also be doing. The garden had now become too small an area for him and he took to wandering further afield, but always returning to be fed. One day I could not find him anywhere. I searched all his secret hiding places, but there was no sign of him. It was on the forest edge that I eventually discovered him, and he was hanging upside down from the top wire of the fence.

He was alive, but his right hind leg was badly hurt. He must have tried to jump the fence, and caught it in the top strand. In the wild this kind of accident is not uncommon, and both roe and red deer can come to grief in this way. Unless someone comes across them, or they manage to release themselves, they will hang until they die. I released him as gently as possible and examined the leg. It was broken just above the elbow and was a clean break. He showed no obvious signs of distress, standing quietly with the broken limb dangling. Even when I took the leg and felt the break, he made no move to escape. In my experience, it is quite astonishing the degree of pain an animal will suffer without making a sound.

The young buck was badly hurt and I felt doubtful about his prospects. Then I remembered a female badger which had been brought to me. She had been caught in a snare and in her struggles to escape, the wire had cut right through the chest wall. This gaping wound was so wide that one could see right into the chest cavity. She, like my buck, had uttered no sound of anguish. It had looked pretty hopeless, but I took her to the vet and asked him to stitch the wound. He shook his head at both the seriousness of the wound, and at a madman wishing to attempt the saving of a wild animal's life. At my insistence, he made as good a job as he could; and indeed it was a good job, for the animal made a complete recovery and eventually was able to return to the wild. When I turned up again, this time with an injured fawn, he again raised his eyebrows; but he had been so pleased with his previous success, that he set to with enthusiasm to make a good job of Bounce. This he did by carefully setting the broken limb in plaster.

For six weeks Bounce was a comical sight. His plaster must have weighed all of six pounds, and at first he limped around, a very subdued little buck. As the time passed, the plaster began to cause an itch, and I felt sorry for him as he tried frantically to scratch the offending irritation. His activity, though, was surprisingly little reduced, and the heavy plaster did not appear to cause him too much discomfort. Cassius used it, most happily, as a rubbing post. There were comical results, too, when in due course it was taken off. Whilst carrying the plaster, he had compensated for the extra weight by leaning to one side. Unconsciously he continued to do the same thing, and there were several ungainly falls. It took him a few attempts to get it right, but once he did, there was no evidence at all that his leg had ever been broken. In the wild, a broken leg will often mend naturally, but the limb will not be straight. Bounce was lucky.

September ran into October, with its consequent change to his winter coat. A roe deer winter coat is greyish in colour and much thicker in texture than his summer one. The first sign of a change was the breaking of the hair around his neck, as though it had been cut with scissors. His coat began to look patchy and moth eaten. Within a month, however, he had completed the change and was resplendent in dense grey fur, with prominent throat bands of lighter hair. It was a marvellous feeling to run one's fingers through the coat, and to feel its wiry texture.

Except for the odd occasion, Bounce had now stopped taking milk. In the wild, roe fawns stop suckling their mothers at this time, but their red cousins continue to take milk right through winter and into the following spring. Bounce was now living almost entirely on vegetable matter, supplemented with rabbit and calf pellets. He was particularly fond of bramble and ivy leaves, and these, too, are favourite food of his brothers in the wild. For all that he was weaned, he continued to be as friendly as ever.

During the first week of November, I saw the beginning of his antler growth. Two velvet-covered buttons appeared between his ears, and these eventually grew until they were one inch in length. In February, he would rub them off, leaving a temporary scar. The sequence of antler growth in young deer is different to that of adults. The adult buck casts his previous year's antlers in early November, and his new set begins to grow from that time. By the following spring they have become sharp prongs. During the growing period, the immature bone is protected by skin called velvet, and this supplies the growing bone with nutrient. A young fawn does not cast his first buttons until February, and only then does his first true head begin to grow. Normally this is composed of single spikes, unlike the adult, who grows a six point head.

Because of the extra feeding that I had given the little buck, his head, by the following July, was bigger than the average for a

The devastation that was advancing

The old Caledonian forest

In it were four very fine youngsters (*Raven*)

We started to get . . . the cover on (*Don at hide*)

She tore off titbits to feed to her family (*Sparrowhawk and young*)

Standing underneath it . . . when
the rain poured down (*Sparrowhawk and brolly*)

This nest was in an oak, and all of forty feet up (*Buzzard at nest*)

Bouncing on stiff yellow legs (*Young buzzard*)

yearling, and had nearly an adult complement of points. He was bigger and heavier than normal, too, and I knew that he would have to be watched carefully. This was the season of the rut, and I was interested to see what might happen, for there were many roe deer in the nearby forest. I heightened his fence, just in case. Sure enough, one night a wild buck came out of the forest to challenge him. They fought, intermittently, all night, with only the fence between them. By morning, their powerful necks and heads had torn a great hole in the netting, and both had gone.

I guessed that Bounce would come back to be fed, but he would possibly be aggressive and wild. He had once before caught me unawares, and I knew the power of that neck, and the sharpness of those antler points. Once he is weaned, the relationship between a tame buck and his human "mother" changes. Now, he looks on any human being not as a friend, but as a competitor; for in his eyes the human is simply another buck over whom he must assert supremacy. And so, if you are rearing a buck, you will have to assert your authority and show him who is master. This is best done by striking the animal with a switch on the most tender part of his body, namely the nose. Once he realises that you are a stronger "buck" than he is, his challenge will end, and he will revert to his former subordinate role.

Unfortunately, on this occasion, Bounce chose to return by the one road which we were not watching, and he met a local woman on her way to work. She knew him, but knew nothing of what had happened and did not understand his present mood. When she greeted him in the usual fashion, she got a rude surprise. With head lowered aggressively, he charged her, knocking her to the ground. With his antlers, he pinned her there by the leg. Luckily, someone was near at hand and heard her cry for help, and luckily, too, her leg had not been gored by the antlers, only pinned to the ground.

The young buck was quickly recaptured, and indeed, by that time had already reverted to his normal good-natured self. I felt, though, that some plan for his future would have to be made. Ideally one would like to have released him back into the wild, but contact with human beings had continued too long and had formed too strong a bond. One day, perhaps in defence of his territory, he might injure someone; or worse still, trusting a human being, he might fall easy prey to a sportsman's gun. On the other hand, to keep him confined in a small enclosure would be cruelty. In the end I had him tranquillised, and shipped him off to a deer park, where he would be amongst his own kind and have a reasonable amount of freedom.

The moral of this tale must be that no matter how delicate and appealing a roe fawn, or any other wild animal may be, it should be left alone for its own mother to rear, if possible. All become problems, greater or smaller, once they are adult.

Roe deer have always been part of the forest fauna; we know that their bones have been found in Mesolithic middens. The spread of the new forests has helped tremendously by providing a continuation of their natural habitat, ensuring both shelter and food supply. As well as looking after trees, a forester has many other responsibilities, and one of the most important is the welfare of the birds and animals that live in his forest. Some of them are helpful to the growth of the forest, some are not. Blackgame, for example, are very fond of young buds, and especially during the winter can do quite severe damage, thus retarding the growth of the trees. This does not mean, however, that every blackcock and greyhen must necessarily be destroyed. Not so long ago, most foresters would have reacted in exactly that fashion. They held a grudge against all living things that could damage their trees, and quite literally believed that the only remedy was the extermination of the guilty species.

A much more enlightened view is held by most foresters nowadays. It is utterly impossible to grow a forest without some kind of damage being incurred, and all that is necessary is to accept this concept, and to understand that it is often dangerous, in the long term, to upset delicate ecological balances. A forest is much more than a collection of trees; it is a viable entity, with a full complement of living things. A forest containing no living creatures would be a sterile place, and indeed, could not survive anyway. Roe deer, in spite of the damage they sometimes do, are part of the forest, and in fact, are part of the crop obtained from it and should be treated as such.

I began to look at roe deer, in relation to trees, a long time ago and discovered that the damage they do is directly related to the policy adopted towards them. If their way of life is upset by harrying, and the culling of the wrong animals, then much more, not less, damage is done to the trees. They are strongly territorial animals, each territory being held by the strongest bucks. The less these animals are harassed, and their normal way of life disturbed, the less the damage they do to the trees.

Many people, even nowadays and in spite of a growing knowledge of wildlife gained from excellent television programmes, have the idea that animals wander about aimlessly picking up both food and partners, all quite by chance. Nothing could be further from the truth. Some are tied loosely to their habitat, some very tightly. Roe bucks have quite definite territorial boundaries, and defend them from other bucks. The boundaries are influenced by the availability of food, and the power of the male to defend his territory. Master bucks mark their territory by rubbing scent from a gland on the forehead, and at the same time marking the tree with their antlers. Every other buck will understand this message, and the territory holder will have a built-in advantage whilst on his own territory even though he may be weaker than the challenger.

Another buck that I reared, who, like Bounce, also became quite a problem, illustrated this point. When he grew to be unmanageable, I made him an enclosure in the forest, big enough to give him reasonable freedom and scope to live a normal life. In the July of his second year, another buck somehow managed to leap into the enclosure from a high point close beside it. He was unable to get out again, but though he was a much bigger animal and obviously the master buck of the surrounding territory, he could not assert his supremacy over the owner of this area. He found himself confined to one small corner of the enclosure, and not allowed to wander at will around it. Now, he was the intruder upon another's territory, and had to give way. I repeatedly saw the younger animal butt the older, driving him back to his corner. Unable to escape, the buck's position eventually became intolerable, and I freed him.

57

Roe deer are diurnal animals, and therefore tend to come out to feed at dawn and dusk. Because they are territorial in habit it becomes fairly easy to choose a spot where they can be studied, but one has to be out before dawn, and in position before the animals come out of cover to feed. The most likely spot for success is on the edge of a plantation, where there is either open hillside, or where the trees are smaller. A small ladder set against a tree will give sufficient height to avoid the roe deer's sensitive nose.

Rising at four o'clock on a June morning is not too difficult, when the eastern sky is already softly suffused with pink, and a slight breeze holds promise of a midge-free morning. So it was, one early morning, when I went to watch a likely spot on a hillside in my forest. The main tree-line filtered out into a crop of younger trees, and it was an ideal place for roe deer. The old trees would give cover during the day, and there was plenty of sweet grass and herbage for grazing, among the small trees. It was very dark in the forest as I climbed quietly to my perch in the tree. Built against the backcloth of the wood, it could not be easily seen.

It was nearly five before I got settled in, and dawn was not far away. I could see up to the head of the loch, and the dark mass of Cruachan behind it. I knew that the sun, when it rose, would first appear just to the east of the mountain. The world was at the threshold of another day, and a rising tide of pink suffused the rippling waters of the loch. There was still no sign of roe, although they could well be feeding out of sight.

At last, the flaming hoop of the sun rose above the mountain, its face mottled with the wispy streaks of yesterday's cloud. Red and pink fought for supremacy as the flow spread higher across the heavens, filling the loch with unearthly reflections. Suddenly, the dark silhouette of a short-eared owl flew, with high flapping wings, directly over the centre of that glowing ball of flame, and was quickly lost in the dark shadow of the forest. I was so absorbed by the glory of the morning, the changing colours, the silhouette of Cruachan against the eastern sky, that I completely forgot my reason for being there. I could only watch, spellbound, the birth of a new day.

A buck had already started his day. There he was, just discernable in shadow, grazing his way gradually into the open. The rays of the sun picked out the red in his coat. Every few seconds, he warily lifted his fine head before lowering the dark muzzle once more into the rich herbage. A small birch took his fancy, and he nibbled off a few succulent leaves. Next, a willow bush encouraged him to rub an itchy antler, whose light colour indicated that it was newly cleaned of velvet. Through my binoculars I could see a touch of moisture on his coat, the remains of the frosty mantle that covered him overnight, even though it was now nearly midsummer. As he grazed further into the open, I searched around for his doe. Eventually, I spotted her, but a long way off. It was unlikely the two of them would come together this morning.

By six thirty the light was brilliant, with sharp shadows, and already a warmth in the sun. I wanted a picture of the buck, and was afraid that he might take a different path back to his daytime cover among the large trees. Gradually, he grazed his way to the boundary of his territory. Beyond, I was suddenly aware of the silhouette of a neighbouring buck. Both started to show signs of displeasure. Heads were shaken and lowered, and each stared long and hard at the other, across an invisible boundary. Eventually, my buck retreated towards the shelter of the bigger trees. With the sun now behind me, and my 300 mm lens trained on him, I was able to "shoot". He heard the shutter click, even at thirty yards, and lifted his head sharply. With the wind in my favour, and being above him in my tree, no alien scent reached his keen nose. Nevertheless, he was deeply suspicious, and moved away quickly into the sanctuary of the wood. As I climbed stiffly down, a curlew welcomed another day with one of its haunting cries.

The distended flank and belly of the doe that I had glimpsed in the distance, suggested that she had still to drop her young. Roe fawns are always born somewhere within the territory of their parents, and June is normally the month. The weather, for June, was foul, with misty rain and dripping foliage making it difficult to sight any animals. On several visits, I searched the likely spots. You would think that this was an impossible job, but knowing the habits of the animals does make it possible to eliminate certain areas. A roe doe does not have her young in the dark depths of the forest, but she chooses a more open area with light cover in the form of deep heather, bracken, or just small trees. The youngsters get the full benefit of the sun and sufficient shelter from wind and rain when it comes, but are safely away from the continuous drip of the larger trees when they shed heavy rain or dew.

Early one afternoon, when there was scattered cloud and the sun only occasionally peeped through, I set off once again to search. This time I took my labrador. I chose the open area where I had previously watched the animals, and dividing it into sections, combed it thoroughly. The trees were three feet tall, and there was a deep covering of heather. Little birches and willow bushes contrasted sharply with the dark green of spruce behind. Shuna ranged from left to right with busy nose, used to this business and very efficient. She found.

The fawn lay quietly below a small spruce, and was surrounded by a protecting wall of heather. The spotted coat, although startling in its brilliance, merged well with the broken pattern of the vegetation. The head was stretched along its flank, and it lay absolutely motionless. Shuna stood motionless too, seemingly as entranced as I was. I knelt beside it and murmured gently to it, and then touched the glossy coat with one finger. It was like the finest silk, and I had to restrain an almost irresistible urge to pick it up. I quickly took a photograph, sexed it, marked the spot with a piece of coloured tape tied to a nearby bush, then moved off to search for another. Usually, roe have twins, and sometimes triplets, and it was no surprise, therefore, when the dog found another some thirty yards away.

Next morning, I was back on my stance in the tree to watch for the doe when she fed her young. The trees wept with summer rain, and my seat was uncomfortable. Drips fell monotonously on my head, and by seven I was nearly giving up. Suddenly, like a wraith in the mist, she appeared from the wood, and in little bounds approached the spot that I had marked. I could clearly see her full udder. She paused just a moment before taking the final step, then lay down. Because of the vegetation, I could see neither of them, but having felt the hard pull of a fawn on my finger, I could guess what was happening. It took ten minutes to satisfy this one, and when the doe rose, I expected her to go to the other. Instead, she drifted away in the opposite direction, and I guessed that the worst had happened. When she was out of sight, I investigated. Sure enough there was no sign of the other fawn, except for a hollow in the heather. A strong smell of fox was still in the air, and it was obvious that another of nature's inexorable laws had been fulfilled.

The welfare and husbandry of deer form an important part of a forester's job. They multiply rapidly, and if care is not taken they harm not only their habitat, but also do harm to themselves by continual battling over territory. Because forests are fenced off from neighbouring land, deer are, in a sense, prisoners within the woodlands, and their numbers require controlling. Provided this is done in a humane and selective manner, and in the correct season, a viable and useful stock can be built up. It is by proper and selective culling that the quality of the stock can be improved. A census of the beasts is taken and a percentage of the animals is then shot. This number might vary between twenty and thirty per cent, and the poorer quality stock is selected.

Clean shooting is the ideal control, and though the only shooting that I do is with a camera, there is a tremendous thrill to be experienced in stalking these animals. The advantage lies perhaps with the beast, but man pits his knowledge and reasoning power against the instinct and amazing powers of scenting, hearing and sight of the deer. Using a camera is much more difficult than using a gun. The same tactics of stalking are employed, but with the camera it is necessary to get much closer to the target. At the crucial moment, the rifle can be pushed through the vegetation, but the camera must be brought to eye level, and this means lifting the head.

A recently developed method of shooting is from a high seat built in a tree, or on a platform of steel. The advantages are that the shooter aims towards the ground, so lessening the chances of hurting anyone; and the target is more easily seen. It is questionable whether sportsmen get the same satisfaction from this kind of shooting. I know that a wildlife photographer does not.

Spring Fever

One early morning in the middle of March, I was sitting in my "den" thinking about the day's work ahead. It was a typical spring morning, and such mornings always coax me quickly from my bed. Overnight there had been a hard frost, and this had consolidated, for at least another day's delight, previous falls of snow upon the surrounding hills. The sun was beginning to find its way into the narrow valley, and swirling patches of mist were rising from the loch. Trees, hedges, plants, grasses, all sparkled in their frosty mantles, and I decided to make my way down to the lochside before breakfast, to catch the sparkle and the mist with my camera.

It was good to be alive. There was that indefinable something in the air that heralds the approach of another season. I could see early buds on bushes and trees, and the frost-encrusted branches of hazel were adorned with graceful yellow tassels. I became aware that blackbird, mavis, robin and hedgesparrow were all singing out their hearts, staking territorial claims, attracting mates, or maybe just feeling full of the joys of spring. Jackdaws were busy foraging in the field in front of the house, and they reminded me of

Kilmartin days when their presence was very much a part of the springtime scene.

It was at home in Kilmartin that my father gave me what was, perhaps, my first conscious lesson in birdwatching. Normally, jackdaws nest in holes on cliff faces, or when enough of these are not available, in shallow depressions on the ground. But our birds preferred the tall red brick chimneys of some of the village buildings, and great was the activity as they strutted importantly around looking for nest-building material. Accomplished thieves at all times, their beady eyes missed nothing, and many strange bits and pieces were collected together at this time. One day, my father pointed out to me the interesting technique used by the birds to build their nests in the chimneys. A bird would carry small twigs to the top, then drop them as nearly horizontal as possible down the chimney. It was not long before a stick would jam, and others soon be caught. Soon a platform would be formed upon which the nest proper could be built. The younger birds took longer to learn this trick, and many a stick fell right down the chimney into pots and pans on the fire below.

This early experience in observing bird behaviour also gave me my love for this particular family of birds, and now, as I returned to the house for breakfast, I decided once again to include its largest member, the raven, in my plans for the coming season's photography.

I like to find for myself the birds and animals that I wish to study and photograph, since it gives a great deal more satisfaction than if someone else has done all the preparatory work. When the animal or bird has been found for one, and the work of building hides done by someone else, it all becomes a rather mechanical exercise, with no feeling of personal involvement. But this personal involvement will mean, however, that one will have to be satisfied with only a very few subjects in any one season.

When I am first appointed to a new area, I spend my first winter there exploring all the possibilities. My job, in any case, requires that the new forest is reconnoitred and studied, but most weekends, when the weather is reasonable, I walk the likely places in forest and wood, and on the surrounding hills. At that time of the year, when trees are bare, and rocks unencumbered with summer vegetation, old nesting sites are easily discovered, and will give one a good idea of where to look the following season.

This spring, in addition to the raven, I decided to concentrate on short-eared owl, hen harrier, buzzard and sparrowhawk, and wrote off for the necessary licences. This was a fairly full programme, and much would depend on how easily each pair and its nest was located, as to whether or not it was completed. I had a friend, Budge Cavenaugh, who was anxious to have the experience of a full season's study of these birds, and with his help in watching and seeing me in and out of hides, it should be easier. I checked that he was able and willing, and arranged to 'phone him nearer the time to get started. Meantime, I spent most spare moments sorting out material for the various hides that we would require.

There was a previous occasion when I had prided myself upon my forethought in the matter of hide-building. I had found a very good raven's nest with young in it ready to fly. It was too late to attempt photography that season, but surely they would nest again in such a perfect situation next year. I would build my hide as soon as the youngsters had flown, and it would be ready for me, and the birds used to it, by the crucial time next season. It presented quite a challenge, in that the only possible place for a hide was on a narrow ledge halfway down the rock face, and the only way of reaching it was by using a rope. With great enthusiasm I climbed that rope a great many times, festooned with all the bits and pieces necessary for the job. I was quite proud of the finished article. It had stout walls of planking and a waterproof roof to shield me from the biting winds of March and April. We had some severe gales that winter, and my marvellous construction stood up to them all. But, the ravens' nest did not! Every stick of it was blown away, and they built themselves a new one. It was only a few feet below the old, but was quite useless from the point of view of photography.

Nowadays, my hides are kept firmly stowed away until they are needed. In my garage, and usually to the discomfort of my car, there is a marvellous assortment of odds and ends which I am sure will come in useful one day. The basic requirements for a hide are four legs and a cover, but it is seldom that its positioning will allow legs of all the same length, and the cover has to be one that will blend perfectly with the surroundings. So, I have a great collection of poles and sticks of varying lengths, and as many different covers as I can manage. Old camping material is particularly suitable, but no offerings are ever turned away.

The covers, in particular, suffer a great deal of abuse. They get a fresh chopping around every time they are used, for the camera has to be carefully aligned with the subject, and the lens hole for the previous session, together with its accompanying peepholes, never seems to be suitable. Scissors and a large packet of safety pins are a "must" on each and every expedition.

Many drunken-looking edifices are the consequence of the peculiar needs of each situation. On uneven ground you may end up with a hide with legs each of a different length, the cover weirdly draped to accommodate their uneven placing. On a cliff face the hide may have to be precariously secured by means of ropes and tent pegs to pockets of soil, or convenient boulders.

Perhaps the most splendid of all the hides are those built for photographing sparrowhawks. The nest will probably be high in a larch tree, and three slim poles are used in conjunction with one of the trees, to form a pylon. Short lengths of wood are used to couple them together for the full height of the construction. These struts form a ladder to the platform which is laid at the top, and on this the hide is placed. It is a very pleasant experience to perch there high above the larch wood. So, also, thought a tawny owl. One recently made use of the platform of one of my old hides as a nesting site. Unfortunately, her two eggs did not hatch. Perhaps it had been too draughty.

By mid April, Budge and I were ready. Hide materials had been sorted out and cameras checked after the winter. I was fairly certain I knew where a raven might be nesting, and one Saturday morning we set out for a nearby cliff to look for it. I carried a bundle of posts for a hide, and we took cameras, just in case something turned up.

It was a marvellous day, and we hastened up through the forest to get out on to the open hill as quickly as possible. Moving quietly, the wind in our faces, we surprised a buck and his doe daintily nibbling the herbage in a clearing. They vanished quickly, effort-lessly bounding over young spruce and pine, giving us a splendid view of startled ears and white kidney-shaped rumps, and we could hear the sharp barks of the buck for some minutes afterwards. Then, as we walked the top road of the forest, we suddenly froze in our tracks. A hundred yards ahead, a hind came up from the forest below, to cross the road to the trees above. She was followed by about thirty others, graceful, stiffly-stepping creatures who gave us a startled glance from dark, gentle eyes, then hurried after their sisters to the shelter of the pines above. Budge was so surprised and delighted that he forgot to try for some photographs.

Out on the open hill, we reluctantly decided not to be tempted by little groups of hinds glimpsed briefly on ridge and in hollow, but pressed on towards our cliff as fast as possible. I found myself noting that the vegetation was extremely dry, and remembered that the wind had been easterly for some days. This is the forester's nightmare time of year, when fires are easily started and emergencies can occur with horrifying rapidity. Though not on duty, I would not be far, nor long, from base, and I could be contacted immediately by radio should an emergency arise.

A short time before we reached the cliff, we heard the deep "kronk, kronk" of adult ravens. Evidently they had a look-out post from which they had seen us. As we approached the top, we saw them gliding down the glen together, in leisurely majesty, occasionally talking to each other. When they came to the loch, they wheeled sharply round the hillside, and returned to take a look at us. Breasting the north easterly wind, they seemed to float on it with consummate ease as they inspected us. Then they flew across the glen to alight on rocks the other side, and as we began our exploration, we could hear them calling to each other from time to time.

It was a good cliff. The escarpment stretched for perhaps a quarter of a mile, and faced south east. The top hundred feet or so were extremely steep and rocky, quite difficult of access, but beneath it, loose boulders gradually replaced solid rock, eventually becoming a long scree slope sliding into the young forest below.

66

Even on the steepest section, little crevices and gullies supported enough soil for ferns, grass, and plants to grow, and from one or two fissures near the top, rowan trees braved the exposed conditions. There were a number of rock ledges, and it was upon one of these that we found our nest.

It was about thirty feet from the top, under an overhang, and marvellously constructed. The ledge sloped steeply outwards, and the ravens had built what looked like a giant swallow's nest, so precariously was it stuck to the rock. It was, in fact, anything but precarious, for in it were four very fine youngsters who were perfectly safe. There they were, all with mouths agape, waiting to be fed by their parents. The deep salmon pink of their mouths was startling in contrast with the immature grey of their plumage.

It looked like being a good position for photography, with a possibility of sunshine on the nest until the early afternoon, and we looked to see if there was anywhere a hide could be placed. A grassy ledge, which sloped slightly outwards, might do. It was about twenty feet from the nest, and though a small rowan clung to the cliff midway between ledge and nest, it did not obstruct vision. The way down was steep and rather wet, but by and large I reckoned it would have to do. There was nowhere else suitable anyway.

I placed the bundle of hide posts on the ledge, and we withdrew to wait in a convenient hollow behind a boulder. If the adult birds would not accept the bundle I would have to retrieve it and try again later. We were lucky, for the female soon returned with food for her family. She flew in with no hesitation at all, and I did not think she would be much worried by the completed hide.

When the hen had had a reasonable time with her chicks, we went down to the ledge again. On this occasion we erected the posts, holding them in position by means of ropes to tent pegs and convenient boulders. Then we hung the struts all over with large pieces of heather. The youngsters were not old enough to exhibit much alarm at our presence, but crowded together, heads down under bodies or wings, an occasional bright beady eye could be seen regarding us.

Once again we retreated, and to our delight we did not have long to wait. The female again returned with food. She banked steeply

67

in alarm when she saw the heather hide, then flew to a nearby rock to consider the situation. Deciding there was nothing to fear, she glided in to the nest. We could now start for home. Weather permitting, we planned to be back again next morning.

Complete with hide cover, scissors and safety pins, tripod and cameras, we were back again the next day around nine o'clock. I noticed that the sun was already on the nest, and that an overhang of rock might cause it to be in shadow within a few hours. The young family was well. Yesterday's disturbance had been of no consequence. We got busy at once.

Budge, stretched full length on his stomach, handed down the cameras and tripod over the last difficult bit, and gently dropped the cover. He followed me down and we started to get the heather off the framework, and the cover on. We worked as quickly as possible, for I was not sure about the sun, and I planned to work with both colour film and black and white. The idea was that Budge would go to yesterday's convenient boulder to watch what happened. If the birds accepted the completed hide, then he would leave the area at a suitable moment when the adults had departed again for more food. But if they did not accept it, then he would come back for me immediately, and we would take the cover off and make another attempt on some other day.

At last all was fixed up and I was settled in. Budge departed, and I waited to see what would happen. No matter how often one has this experience, the excitement never varies. There is a tingling down the spine, and nerves are taut with anticipation. Ears are cocked to catch the slightest sound, and all sounds must be quickly identified. Is that the rush of air through wing pinions, as a bird comes flying in? Is that a bird hopping cautiously from branch to branch, or from rock to rock, as it approaches the nest? Are the youngsters suddenly alert, knowing that an adult is about to arrive with food? And, after a long period of no action at all, where have those wretched birds got to? Is anything wrong? Have they detected some slight movement, or heard a sound that frightened them? Will one have to hastily withdraw, complete with camera equipment and hide, in case an anxious hen deserts either eggs or chicks?

Generally speaking, it is moments of action that one wishes to catch with the camera, and so one hopes that the adults will not be long away from the nest. The larger the species, the longer the period away as a rule, and the more nerve-racking the task of photography, for opportunities will be few and far between. A little wagtail will return every few minutes with a beakful of insects, but a buzzard or eagle, if her family is well grown, may only pay one visit with food during all the hours of daylight. Usually a hen sitting on eggs will return to sit fairly quickly if she is unworried by the hide. One must be ready for the moment, for it may be hours before she will leave again. If she is brooding chicks, she may decide to shelter them from sun or rain. She may stay put for quite a while, and there is no action to photograph. So the tension mounts. One is keyed up to catch moments of action, but also to avoid disturbing a bird that might desert.

It began to be very warm in the hide, for as so often happens in Scotland, the spring weather was what the summer's should be and seldom is. A few flies buzzed around the roof, an early bee explored the surrounding vegetation, and it was nice to know that as yet it was too early for midges. The young birds in the nest lay quietly, panting a little. A little preening was done from time to time, but mostly they slept.

Suddenly, as if warned by some unseen messenger, they all sprang to life. Heads were turned skywards and mouths opened wide, pink vacuums at the top of grey-black flasks, waiting to be filled. There was a rush of wing beats, a crescendo of cheeps from the chicks, and the hen alighted on the edge of the ledge. I pressed the shutter release and wound on quickly for the next picture. With no waste of time, and not even a glance at the hide, she hopped to the edge of the nest. I shot again. There followed a hectic moment or two while the meal was regurgitated by the hen, the hungry family clamouring all the while. Then she took off, lazily turning over into the air and out of my sight. I hoped that Budge had seen her and would depart from the area.

For a little while there was much activity at the nest. After the meal, a good preening was necessary, and beaks were drawn through wing feathers and backs also carefully worked over. Two waddled clear of the others to do some experimental wing-flapping. So energetic was one that he almost fell overboard. These youngsters were developing fast, and I reckoned that this would probably be our only opportunity for photography. They would soon leave the nest. But, for the moment, they were content to settle down again. A little re-shuffling of bodies and wings to get comfortable, an occasional bright eye cast skywards, and then all were asleep.

I had arranged for Budge to return in three hours, and during this time I was able to photograph various activities, trying for different pictures each time. First, I shot in colour while the light was good, and then went on to black and white. Around half past twelve I heard a whistle approaching, and then Budge's enquiring voice from somewhere above. He decided not to take my place in the hide, for the nest was already in shadow. We left the young ravens regretfully, knowing it was unlikely we would see them in the nest again.

That evening, over a pint, I told Budge of my favourite raven of all. I had found her at the bottom of a cliff, a youngster that had fallen out of the nest. She was strutting around uneasily, apparently unhurt but unable as yet to fly. The nest was quite unreachable, so I took her home. It was not my intention to tame her, but simply to see that she survived until able to fend for herself. But "Cronk" became very domesticated, a great character who gave me endless amusement.

She was an excellent mimic. Each morning, I was awakened by barks coming from the top of a chimney. They reverberated round the house, and I knew it could not be Shuna, the labrador. There was no respite at all until I opened the back door. Then the noise ceased, for there she was already, down from her chimney top and waiting to hop over the doorstep for some fun. She had come to breakfast among other things. Her first ploy was to hop straight up on to the table to sample the butter, the sugar, and the milk, all of them becoming mixed together upon her beak and inserted into the next item that might take her fancy.

Then she considered her next piece of mischief, and this might be successfully making off with the latest object that she coveted. Like all of her kind, she liked to steal things and hoard them. Nothing was

70

Carrion crows at a sheep carcase

I would hear Cronk . . . with the local hoodies (*Hoodie at nest*)

A curlew had made her nest (*Curlew at nest*)

Wonderful camouflage to blend with...their habitat (*Young curlew*)

sacred, and when I was away from home, windows had to be firmly closed. The oddest things tempted her. Glass ashtrays, combs, anything bright, and even cakes of soap, all appealed to her and might be found by me many months later when digging the garden.

Having been foiled in the matter of thieving, Cronk might next consider teasing the dog or the cat. Shuna, the most placid of creatures, was reasonably free of her attentions. An odd nip or two was all that she had to endure. Cassius was a totally different matter. His catty nature was not so sweet, and he could soon be provoked into spitting and hissing and arching his back, manifestations which Cronk seemed to find highly diverting. Eventually, the cat was driven to seek refuge in the garden.

Cronk was great fun to take for a walk. She always accompanied me and Shuna when we went into the forest, and hopped along beside us most companionably. Then, suddenly and silently, she would take off, rejecting human company for the moment and seeking that of her kind. I would hear her playing with the local hoodies, with whom she was great friends, and would catch sight of her in grand aerial displays and mock battles. Sometimes she met the local pair of buzzards, and they thought her very odd, for she barked at them rather as Shuna might have done. On these forest expeditions, she never lost me. Whenever I appeared in a clearing, down she swooped to perch on my shoulder and tell me of her latest adventures.

One day, a neighbour came out to buy something from the local grocery van. The woman suddenly remembered that she needed something from the house. Putting her purse on a windowsill, she went back inside to fetch it, and Cronk seized this opportunity to demonstrate her ingenuity as a thief. From nowhere she materialised beside the purse, considered it a moment, opened it with her beak, and was only prevented from making off with a neatly rolled five pound note, by its irate owner arriving in the nick of time. Upraised arms and an indignant shout caused Cronk to drop her booty, mostly from surprise, I suspect.

When springtime came, Cronk was filled with the urge to build a nest, and she chose the narrow windowsill of an upstairs room. It must have seemed the ideal spot to her, but she had reckoned

71

without the slope. Sticks were carefully laid, one upon the other, arranged with painstaking precision, the nucleus of a platform upon which the nest would be built. But she never got beyond the foundations of her building. As soon as a fair number of sticks had been carefully arranged, the whole bundle slid inexorably off the sloping sill. Again and again, the patient Cronk flew down to retrieve her sticks, becoming more and more frustrated and cross. In the end she gave up the unequal struggle and acknowledged defeat.

The following spring, when similar urges again attacked Cronk, she forsook her unsatisfactory windowsill, and made off over the forest and far away to the hills in the west. Presumably she found a mate, for I never saw her again.

First Find Your Bird

We were now into the second half of April, and the next few weeks were very busy. There was no second chance to photograph raven, but the nests of hen harrier, buzzard, sparrowhawk and short-eared owl had all still to be found. It was a time of watching, with eyes perpetually searching the skies, ears always cocked for certain calls, and binoculars ever ready, their straps wearing a permanent groove into the backs of our necks.

Sometimes we worked together, and this made the job quite a lot easier, for often there were two birds in the air at the one time, and one could watch the hen while the other kept the cock in view. During the breeding season there is always activity of one sort or another that will give a clue to the position of the nest one is looking for. A cock may return with food for the hen, who is sitting on eggs, or both parents will be busy trying to keep a young family satisfied.

Our searches took us to many different places: to forest areas and young plantations, to hills and ridges, and to rocky gullies. Sometimes we could use a car and were able to sit in great comfort looking for our quarry. Often we had to tramp to some high vantage point from where it was possible to see over a wide area. Sometimes I was lucky enough, when out about my business in the forest, to catch sight of promising action that could be investigated later.

That was the watching part of the game. Then came the walking. When we thought we had found the position of a nest, it was then a matter of quartering all sorts of different types of terrain to find the exact spot. The larch woods, looking for sparrowhawk, were the most pleasant. Springy grass or moss to walk on, the sun filtering through the high canopy above, and the wind whispering encouragement through the branches, were all marvellous, but young spruce plantations were hard going, with furrows from the original ploughing still to be reckoned with, hidden as they were by a thick growth of heather. An unwary step frequently resulted in an undignified sprawl on to a spiky resting place.

It gets light very early in the morning by the beginning of May, and one day we motored down the lochside to a wide expanse of moorland. Here was a young spruce plantation, and we had previously spotted a pair of short-ears in the vicinity. This is ideal nesting country for both short-ears and harriers, and we were hopeful it would produce something for us. We parked the car in a spot that would give us a wide field of vision, and waited to see what would happen.

It gradually grew lighter in the east, a luminous sky full of pink and gold, and banks of mist giving promise of a fine warm day to follow. Beneath us, in the plantation, a pale shape, with dark face and long rounded wings, flapped slowly over the mist-enshrouded ground. It was a short-eared owl, and shortly afterwards we picked up another. They appeared to be hunting, flying low, coasting over and round the small spruce trees, wraithlike and silent in the early morning haze. They seemed to examine every square foot of ground, sometimes dropping to earth in a sudden pounce, often rising again with nothing. We hoped that one of them would soon catch prey and carry it to the nest. Frequently they flew over or near the car, taking not the slightest notice of it and giving us a wonderful glimpse of pale streaked bodies and wings. Sometimes they rested awhile on a fence post or down on a tussock in the heather, often doing a little preening at the same time.

74

All the bird world was busy. Meadow pipits, chaffinches, black-birds, thrushes and robins filled the air with song, and a large population of curlew sent plaintive cries echoing over the plantation. Blackcock had a lekking ground somewhere to the east, and we could hear their crooning calls bubbling into the morning air. A cuckoo alighted on the fence in front of us. She worked her way along it, from one post to another, carefully examining the ground in the plantation. Now and again she flew down for a closer look, and we reckoned that she was looking for pipits' nests to lay her eggs in. Then she flew on to a young spruce to delicately pull a caterpillar from a branch. This she gobbled most indelicately, before continuing her search for a nest. I reached for the camera that I usually carry, and found it had been forgotten. Another chance missed!

This momentary distraction lost us one of the short-ears, the hen we thought. We could not see her anywhere, and presumably she had caught a vole and was somewhere quietly enjoying it. Perhaps she had flown back to her nest and we had missed a golden opportunity of spotting its position. The cock did not help us either, for soon he disappeared behind a ridge of spruce and did not reappear. And our time had run out. Breakfast and work were calling, and we would have to try another day.

A few mornings later, when Budge had returned to look for short-ears once again, I went up into the forest to see what activity there might be there. In the late evening and the early morning are the best times of day for seeing deer. This morning was no exception. The wind was in my favour, and I passed two or three grassy clearings in which roe deer were feeding. Nibbling delicately at leaves and plants, surprised-looking faces with gentle inquisitive eyes were raised to regard me. Nor were they unduly alarmed, for it was only after several minutes that they thought discretion the better course, vanishing without too much haste into the forest. I remembered that it would not be too long before fawns would be born and we could start looking for one of the most delightful of summer arrivals.

In a forest glade near the top of the hill I sat and watched a buck and doe, my attention totally on their beautiful russet coats and dainty movements, and suddenly I became aware of an increasing crescendo of buzzard calls. It is a sad plaintive cry, and the sound echoed above the forest, filling the air with urgent messages. I was astonished to see no fewer than nine buzzards, all circling slowly and eagle-like against the deep blue of the spring sky. This was the largest concentration that I had ever seen, and I watched fascinated through my glasses as they glided round and round. It seemed to me that they began to come together in pairs, and then gradually each pair was disappearing from the area, their cries slowly diminishing. I did not see what happened to the one bird who would not be able to find a mate, but in five minutes the sky was empty. Territories had evidently been sorted out and mates chosen for another season. I decided to return to this part of the forest later in the month. One of these pairs might well be nesting in it.

On the 7th May I saw a strange bird high ..bove the forest. It was a dry windless morning with promise of fair weather to come, and the sun glinted on its grey plumage as it swooped and circled in joyous abandon. For a moment I could not identify it, but then a larger, brownish bird rose to meet it, and I realised that they were hen harriers. These are wonderful birds to watch. Through the glass I saw them meet face to face, feet outstretched. Like two cardboard cut-outs against the blue sky, they paused briefly before separating, each in a long swooping glide. Again they climbed into the sapphire sky, wheeling in tight circles round each other, and again coming together. I wondered, for a moment, if they were going to mate up there, for this was a mating display, but suddenly they dived steeply to land behind a heather ridge. I marked the spot in my mind, and set off to look for them.

To reach the ridge, I had to climb up through a stand of Douglas fir, and the resinous aroma from its crushed needles clung to my clothes, pungent yet pleasant. I made my way out on to the open hill. Here was a crop of young spruce, but I kept well into the shelter of the Douglas while scanning the hillside ahead. A sharp "peeoo, peeoo" call above me swivelled my head upwards, and I saw the cock. The sun again caught his greyness, and I could see, too, the black at the ends of his pinions. His wings fluttered, and he swayed in typical harrier fashion as he called again.

Below his body his yellow foot held a small dark bundle, and I was immediately alert. There was a sudden movement to my right, a repetitive "kek, kek, kek", the call of the hen, and she rose to meet him. In a brief coming together the food was passed to her. Then, breaking apart, she glided down to land on a heather knoll in front of me. She started to feed, and for a moment I thought her nest was there. But after tearing the prey apart with beak and feet, she took off again, disappearing over the brow of the hill.

The nest must be somewhere close at hand. I decided to stay under cover for a little longer, and it was lucky that I did. In five minutes she was back on the same knoll, and suddenly, the cock called again, appearing like a grey shadow above. He glided down towards her, and with wings outstretched, landed on her to mate, the event lasting no more than five or six seconds. He took off again, soaring into the blue sky, and she shook out her ruffled brown plumage, before flying off to a point near the top of the knoll. This surely must be the position of the nest, for again she remained at the same spot, though I could not see her because of the vegetation. I was soon to have confirmation. A call from her mate echoed across the hillside, and flying low, he glided towards her. In his foot was a bunch of dried molinia, a favourite nest-building material, and this he left with her. I was sure now.

I withdrew quietly downhill, having no wish to disturb her until the clutch was laid. She had probably started, for harriers begin to lay near the end of April or the beginning of May, but I decided to wait a week or two before going back to check on this pair.

Budge, meantime, had been watching the short-ears whenever time permitted, but not with any great success. In fact, these little birds were leading us a merry dance, and it was very difficult to determine just what was going on. One day we decided to try an evening visit to the plantation. It had been a very hot day, the sun blazing out of a cloudless sky, and haze had gradually built up, obscuring the ridge behind and blotting out the distant view ahead. As we took up our customary position, the sun, a fiery red ball in the west, was gradually sinking behind the hill at our backs, making visibility particularly good.

Against the background of young spruce we soon picked out our two owls. Again, both seemed to be hunting, and we settled down to wait. The cock soon disappeared from sight; prey was evidently scarce at this moment, and he would have to go further afield. But the hen did not follow him, and we watched her fly straight across the plantation to alight, finally, near a small spruce in the centre. There she stayed, not rising at all, but preening from time to time. Occasionally some moving object would catch her eye, and she turned her head to examine it. Sometimes she looked skywards, as though searching for her mate. Still she stayed. Perhaps, at last, this was the site of the nest. Budge kept his eye firmly on her, while I looked for the cock. And this was how Budge missed the drama that was now enacted.

With the deceptively lazy wingbeats of the short-ear, the cock came flying in from the west. Steadily he approached, fairly high, and in his talons he carried prey. Suddenly, another bird was streaking its way towards him, from the north. It looked like a hen harrier, and soon I could see that it was. The short-ear flapped on steadily, apparently oblivious of rapidly approaching danger. The harrier flew in swiftly from beneath, neatly took the prey from the other's talons, and disappeared rapidly in the direction from which she had come. It all happened so swiftly, the short-ear putting up no resistance, that I wondered was it possible that the hen harrier had mistaken the owl for her mate, for this had been the normal behaviour for a food pass. The harrier winged her way back towards the ridge above the forest, and the short-ear, apparently un-perturbed, but supperless, flapped slowly on his way. Finally, he came to land beside the hen, and did not leave her. We decided to see if the nest was there.

As we made our way towards the spot, both birds flew off, so giving us another chance to check on the position. We had carefully counted both rows and trees, but in spite of this, the place was difficult to locate. Trees that had not been visible from the road made counting difficult, and gorse and heather in the furrows that lay between each planted row, made everything look quite different. The stony brown earth provided excellent camouflage for these brown-streaked birds and the saucer-like scrape that was their nest. Half an hour's fruitless toothcombing of the area

78

Cock capercaillie at its lek

Black cocks lekking

Female hen harrier landing at the nest

Cock kestrel on the nest

Roe buck in summer coat

Rufus changing into his summer coat

Female sparrow hawk feeding her young

Barn owl feeding her young

convinced us that we had misread the signs. There was no nest.

By the middle of May we were both distinctly tired of the short-ear plantation. It seemed that we knew every tree, bank of heather, and undulation of the ground, and still we had not pinpointed a nest. And at this moment of discouragement, I had a tragedy with buzzards.

Buzzards nest either on rock ledges or in trees. If on the former, it is surprising how accessible the nest may be. If on the latter, the nest will often be very high in the canopy, and impossible to approach. I was hoping that at least one pair of my nine would have chosen a rock ledge, for it would probably be easier to photograph. Favourite sites are up the steep wooded gullies which often bisect Highland hillsides, and I was walking up one of these during the last week of May. The burn glinted in the sunshine, and gurgled on its way down through the trees. Suddenly, a buzzard flew from a rock shelf which overhung the busy stream. She screamed at me and then circled above calling a plaintive objection to my presence. I had not noticed the nest, which was snuggly built upon the shelf, and she had obviously been frightened by my sudden arrival.

Buzzards are extremely shy birds, and will often desert eggs, or young, if disturbed in this way, and when I discovered two very small downclad chicks in the nest, I was very worried. Anxious to avoid a tragedy, I withdrew as quickly as possible and hurried on my way up the hill. I followed the burn through the trees, to be under cover all the time, and this was a stupid mistake. When I returned the next day to check that all was well, I found a couple of dead youngsters, the flies already busy at their work. Beside the nest were the bodies of a male and female weasel, and a frog, all un-touched. There had been no food there the previous day, and I could only surmise that the frantic parents had not seen me leave. By the time they had plucked up courage to feed their family, it was too late.

I felt very sick indeed over this failure, and discouraged too, for I should have known better. In fact, I decided to give up the idea of buzzards for this year. When, however, I accidentally came across another nest, it seemed stupid not to take advantage of it, but I was very, very cautious.

This nest was in an oak, and all of forty feet up. There was a rocky outcrop further up the hillside which was close enough for photography, and would be suitable for a hide. There were two fledglings, and these ones were a few days older. Already there were touches of black in their feathering, and they had started to preen. The adults circled above me, uttering sharp warning cries, and this time I gave them ample opportunity of seeing me leave the area. A few days later, I returned with the material for building the hide, and was delighted to find, safe and sound, two very healthy young birds. There was some food on the nest, though I could not identify it, and on the ground was a dead ewe. No doubt, the buzzards, being scavengers, were using it as a source of supply.

Spring merged into summer, and life became increasingly hectic. The buzzard could be photographed as soon as the hide was completed. The hen harrier would have hatched off by now, and her hide could be started. Budge found a sparrowhawk nest in one of the larch woods, which must be examined as soon as possible. The short-eared owl's nest had still to be located, and time must be found for further visits to the plantation.

The weather became an obsession, and each evening we eagerly checked the forecast, each morning opened apprehensive eyes in case it was pouring rain. Anxious discussions took place. Which bird should we tackle next? Which one was at the stage we wanted for photography? Which one might hatch her eggs at any moment? If there were youngsters, were they close to flying? Should we take time to go and look for the short-ear again? And so on. Time was short for all that had to be done.

High Hawks

The nest that Budge had found was in a larch wood that contained three old nests, and a fourth had been built. It was very quiet in the wood on the day that we went to look at it. Fresh green grass carpeted its floor, silencing our footsteps, and the only sound was the rustling of a gentle breeze in the tops of the trees. We saw no adult bird leave the area, but I could imagine the hen slipping noiselessly away, a grey-brown phantom winging its way through the trees as she heard us coming. Then, as we approached the nesting site, we passed an uprooted larch. I noticed feathers on the ground beneath the upturned roots, and droppings on some of the root branches. This looked like the plucking post of a sparrowhawk cock, and was promising evidence that they were back in this wood again.

The nest that we wanted to examine was forty feet up in the tree, and there were no convenient rock ledges near at hand. The first task was to discover whether it could be reached, and if there were eggs. Larch trees are much more difficult than oak to climb. The branches are extremely brittle, and it is best to act as though one is walking on eggs, moving lightly and quickly, treading delicately, placing one's feet as close to the trunk as possible. I climbed quickly, and arrived at a position from which I could see into the nest. It was the usual rather flat, untidy construction of larch twigs, and in the centre were five blue-white eggs with red-brown blotches. I thought it would be some time yet before they hatched. We could safely leave this bird for a few weeks, and this would enable us to take our time over building the hide. As we left the area, the scolding "kek, kek, kek" of the hen broke the silence, and we caught a fleeting glimpse of a brown bird streaking through the branches as she returned to brood her eggs.

We took nearly three weeks building that hide. Photography would have to be from a larch close-by, and it seemed to me that we must erect a pylon. I chose three slim forty-foot poles, already seasoned, and therefore light in weight. These we took up to the wood, and left on the ground quite close to the nest. This was the first step in accustoming the birds to the changes they would have to get used to. On a second and third visit, we spaced the poles round a larch about twelve feet from the nest, leaning them against convenient branches higher up. On the last trip we coupled them together with struts of wood.

We never stayed long on these visits, though it was very pleasant working in the coolness of the larch wood. Always, as we left, we saw a small hawk against the blue sky, who disappeared into the darkness of the trees, flying swiftly and silently towards her nest. During the period of our building, the eggs had hatched and she now had a young family clamouring to be fed. She was always impatient to return to her brood.

I, too, was becoming impatient, anxious to start photography. And the day, bright and sunny with just a touch of soft wind to cool the air, came at last. Mossy twigs broke sharply beneath our feet as we approached the nest area, and we heard the hen's angry cries as she flew through the trees. Those intruders again! I climbed quickly into the hide, erected the tripod and set up the camera, then called down to Budge that he could leave.

At last all was quiet, the larch wood again a peaceful place. The sun glinted through its branches, the wind whispered in the tree-tops, and it was a marvellous feeling to sit up there with the young hawks. The sun shone straight on to the nest, and the youngsters panted gently. I noticed that their feathering was already mottled with black, their eyes dark and shiny. White down was everywhere, for juvenile coats were being shed. Four of them were able to move about, but the fifth was very small, a motionless bundle in the centre of the platform of twigs. In fact, all the youngsters were of a different size, for like all the hawk family they had hatched off at different intervals. Occasionally, one would shuffle to the edge of the nest, then facing inwards, eject a white stream overboard—the family had been well-trained!

My stand swayed slowly back and forth in the breeze, and the branches of the support tree caused flickering shadows to ripple across the nest. I heard the female before I saw her. She called sharply from somewhere behind me, and the youngsters all lifted their heads and became quite agitated. My hand flew to the shutter release. There was a soft rustle of wings against twigs, and suddenly she was there, her fierce yellow eyes glaring straight at me. Then, as she bent her head to tear the bloody prey apart, I could see the paler colouring of her nape. At the end of the long slim legs, her yellow talons firmly grasped her victim as she tore off titbits to feed to her family. It was a young thrush, I thought, and it soon disappeared down their hungry maws. Occasionally, she swallowed a piece herself.

When the feeding was done, she stood back a little, staring at the youngsters. It was a fierce yet somehow tender look, and they responded to it by crowding up to her. Somewhat reluctantly, it seemed, she shifted her wings to allow them room beneath her, but then settled peacefully again. Ripples of shadow passed across her recumbent body, highlighting then dulling her bright eye. Occasionally, a little head peeked briefly from beneath the wing feathers, and sometimes she shuffled and fluffed out her wings. It was very pleasant to watch this intimate family scene, and time passed quickly.

Fully an hour had gone by when, suddenly, the cock called a plaintive "kee-oo, kee-oo". It was his food call to the hen, and she lifted her head immediately. Then she rose and silently flew, with soft clash of wings against green needle tufts, to his plucking post. I could just see the uprooted larch from a peep-hole in the back of the hide. He was very busy, with sharp movement of head and beak, removing the feathers from a pigeon. He worked with such speed that he was almost hidden in a pale grey cloud which fell to the ground in a shower of feathering.

The hen alighted beside him to collect this offering, and it was then that I dropped my camera. I had run out of film, and was trying to reload whilst watching the cock. The camera fell first on to my anorak then bounced off it to the edge of the platform. The breeze gave the stand a larger sway and it slid over the edge. I listened, horrified, as it bumped its way down to the ground. The hawks, with sharp scolding cries, "kek, kek, kek" flew off into the wood.

This mishap served to prove two things: cameras will often stand up to quite considerable ill-treatment, and some sparrowhawks are not easily frightened! The cushion of needles on the forest floor must have saved my camera, for it was quite undamaged, and though I climbed down to retrieve it and returned to the hide quite openly, the hen flew back very shortly. I was afraid that my sudden emergence would have further alarmed her, but in fact, I soon found that this bird, unlike most of the hawk family, was quite unworried by noises from the hide, and eventually I was able to move in and out without Budge's help.

During the next few weeks we spent many happy hours with this bird and her family. Their antics were very amusing, and it was interesting to watch their development right through to the time when they were ready to leave the nest. Long periods were spent in a huddled heap, sleeping quietly. Then, for no apparent reason they would all begin to shuffle around the nest, sometimes teetering on the edge in an alarming fashion, sometimes preening immature feathering. Little scraps of food were carefully picked over, and awkwardly shaped pieces, like the leg of a thrush, were liable to get stuck halfway down. Then beaks snapped open and shut in frantic gulps, and necks were stretched to their uttermost to force the morsel down.

As they got older, the other woodland birds began to take notice whenever the young hawks wandered on to the surrounding branches. Even at this stage of their lives they were recognised as future enemies, and the local chaffinches would challenge them, dive-bombing and scolding them. When this happened, the little hawks, not yet become fierce adults, cowered on the branches, their heads swivelling round anxiously to watch the attacking birds.

On my last visit, I heard a sound like a clock with indigestion. "Ticky, ticky, tock, tock" it went, and at length I discovered what it was. A red squirrel stood on a branch some yards from the nest. Its tail slowly twitched, as a cat's does, and it chattered away as it stared at the young hawks, sizing up the situation. They regarded him impassively, their yellow eyes staring him out. The squirrel advanced a step or two, tail switching furiously, but it could not quite make up its mind to leap. Then, this attack being unsuccessful, and lacking courage to invade the nest, it whirled around, leaping skywards from branch to branch until finally, it was lost to sight. Perhaps the sparrowhawk nest had been the winter home of this squirrel, for squirrels do sometimes build their dreys on old nests.

I climbed down from the hide for the last time. Soon the young hawks would fly, eventually dispersing to find territories of their own. If they survived the hazards of winter, their parents, next season, might again nest in this wood.

I thought this was the end of our sparrowhawk season, but a week later one of my foresters came to the door with a youngster. It was a very angry, bedraggled little object, and one of its wings was drooping. So far as I could see no great damage had been done, and if we could feed it for a while, it would soon recover and learn to fend for itself. I wondered whether it came from our nest in the larch wood.

"Spawky", as she was promptly christened, though I could only guess at her sex, spent her nights in my garage. Here she roosted on the crossbeams, liberally bespattering the floor with her droppings, but was easy to catch in the morning. We made two perches for her use during the day. One was a portion of a tree trunk into which we knocked a substantial staple. The other was my bird table, borrowed temporarily from its customary visitors, who now kept strictly away. I fitted a jess to one of Spawky's legs, attached a fairly long line to it, and tied this to the staple. Thus she had freedom to try her wings, but was prevented from getting into real trouble. Occasionally, an angry little hawk became hopelessly caught up, having wound the line inextricably around the post or the trunk, but she never suffered any harm and allowed herself to be unwound without too much pecking at the hand that was unravelling her. Bertie, the black cat, accustomed to regard visitors to the bird table with a distinctly predatory eye, if only he could persuade them he was just a harmless object enjoying the sunshine, gave this fierce occupant a distinctly wide berth.

The first problem we had with Spawky was that she had not yet learnt to feed herself, and Budge and I took turns at pushing small morsels of raw meat down her throat. She objected strongly to our well-meant but clumsy efforts. Often her beak had gently to be forced open and the morsels poked far enough to make her swallow. She emerged from these battles unbowed, but with a bloody necklace and a look in her eye which condemned our poor endeavours. She then spent quite a while preening herself, and practising a little wing flapping. We noticed that the injured wing was mending well; it should not prove to be any handicap in the future.

The weather turned very showery, and often there were quite long spells of heavy rain. In the larch woods Spawky would have found all the shelter that she needed, but there was no protecting tree over the bird table. It became an awful nuisance to carry her to and from the garage; besides she objected strongly to being put to bed during the day. So we rigged up an old umbrella. This she took entirely in her stride, standing underneath it with smug expression when the rain poured down, but often preferring its top at other times. The only trouble was that it was slippery, and if she did not find exactly the right position at its apex, first one foot and then the other would begin to slide, and there would be an exasperated flurry of wings while she righted herself.

Spawky grew into a very handsome little hawk. We did not want to tame her, but she was beginning to accept us as part of her normal life. She would perch on arm or hand, and was always carried in this way from garage to perch. A small scrap of meat was left after every feeding session, and quite soon she discovered what

I had never seen a cock hen harrier at the nest before
(*Male hen harrier*)

Flight pictures are the most difficult (*Female hen harrier*)

The youngsters were . . . graduated in size as is normal with asynchronous hatching (*Young harriers*)

With fierce yellow eyes (*Short-eared owl*)

to do with it. It was not long before she was feeding herself. The wing, too, now seemed to be functioning normally. Soon we would be able to release her.

But, she took matters into her own hands. One day Budge was carrying her back to the garage for the night. Perhaps he was a little careless, relaxing his grip a little. Shuna, the labrador, bounced suddenly into view. Spawky uttered her usual disapproving squawk at this happening, for she did not like Shuna, then took off for the nearest spruce. For a moment she regarded the humans below, who were hopefully calling her down, then flew with certain instinct in the direction of the larch wood. We reckoned she could look after herself by now, but a few days later went back to the wood to see what was going on. Shuna came too. As we approached the area, a small sparrowhawk flew over her with harsh, scolding cries, then disappeared from sight amongst the trees.

There was a postscript to this episode. One day, during the following winter, I heard a commotion outside my kitchen window. I hurried to look and was just in time to see a sparrowhawk fly off into the forest. On the path were the scattered feathers of a thrush. Had Spawky been short of prey and remembered a good source of supply?

Buzzard Business

My earlier experience with the first pair of buzzards made me especially cautious when we set off to complete the hide for the second pair that we had found. There must not be another tragedy.

After the first pieces of a hide have been laid near a nest, I never leave the area without making sure that an adult has returned to the nest, and has accepted the change. Every bird knows exactly the position of every natural feature in the vicinity of its nest, and any alteration will be noticed. Even if the bird has returned safely, I generally wake the next morning worrying in case the worst has happened. Sometimes, it has. For no valid reason that one can think of, the parent birds have deserted, and one is confronted by a nest-ful of fly-blown youngsters. There is an appalling sense of guilt, a feeling of utter desolation when a tragedy, such as this, does occur. Questions flood the mind. What went wrong? How were the rules broken? Or if they were not, why on earth did it happen? Sick at heart, one retreats from the scene vowing to do no more of this sort of photography.

Many would say that this is sentimental. When it is a species which is in no danger through falling numbers, the loss of one season's young cannot possibly affect the issue one way or the other, the parents will breed again next year. Nature, certainly, is not in the least sentimental, though the human onlooker sometimes gets this impression from courtship displays. Adult birds do not choose the nest site with loving care, nor consciously have affection for their family. Each bird has an inbuilt clock and calendar which tells it when, how and where to build, and with what materials. Instinctive knowledge, gained entirely unconsciously, dictates the number of eggs laid, and this is often related to the available food supply. Each parent has its appointed tasks in rearing the family, and these are carried out automatically in response to certain stimulii. It even happens that should the female die, in a species where she is entirely responsible for the feeding of the young, the cock will take over her duties, and attempt to rear the family himself. It is not sentiment which prompts this action, but an overwhelming instinct to see that his family survives.

However, when interference by man is responsible for disturbing the natural, but entirely unsentimental pattern, then a link in the complex chain is broken, the balance upset. Then man should feel guilty. If one has been the source of that interference, even unwittingly, and a tragedy has occurred, one remembers for a long time the dead bundles of down, the aimless flying around and the plaintive calling of the adult birds, who perch here and there to rest or preen, but never return to the scene of their disaster.

Our second pair of buzzards behaved like models, though, and we had no trouble with them. On this first visit, we took the framework from the bundle on the ground and erected it as quickly as possible. We hung it over with heather and branches of rowan, then retired hastily to see what would happen. This contrary buzzard hen, unlike the first, was not in the least worried by the unusual structure which had taken shape close to her eyrie. She returned immediately to her nest to settle with her young, and the cock went off to hunt. I had planned several visits to complete the hide, but this totally unworried behaviour on the part of the hen tempted me to finish it on the next trip.

We had a day or two of rather broken weather, April-like in character, and a spell of steady and heavy rain made me think of our several young families, buzzard, sparrowhawk and harrier, all cowering beneath their mothers' wings to keep warm and dry. A really long spell of bad weather can be disastrous at this stage. If the hen has continuously to protect her chicks from it, all the hunting must be done by the cock, and if he is not successful, and there is no break in the bad spell, the hen will become desperate. She, too, will then hunt for food, and a prolonged absence from the nest could mean that the young will die from exposure. During this sort of weather, if a human being should frighten the hen off for a long period, the same unhappy result might obtain.

Our wet spell was followed by a couple of days of showers and bright intervals. The bright intervals became longer and the showers less frequent, and on the fourth day we thought we might risk a visit. It was decided to complete the hide, and instal me inside while Budge hid himself in a cave down the hillside. Here he would be within earshot should I have to whistle. If the birds took fright at the completed structure we would have to restore it to phase two, retreat from the scene and try again on another day.

There was a wonderful freshness in the rain-cleared atmosphere as we climbed the hill to the eyrie. Buds were bursting in the oak wood, and delicate tendrils of green leaf were sprouting. Above us the adult birds circled continuously. Quickly spotting us as we approached the area, they now called with plaintive mewing cries to warn their chicks of danger. Once at the hide, we took a quick look at the youngsters to check that all was well, then hurried to finish it. When complete, with cover on and heather replaced, it did not look so different, and I was hopeful that we would have no difficulty with the adults. Preparations for photography were quickly made, and then Budge departed, hoping to be able to leave me for about three hours.

The buzzard nest rocked gently as the tree swayed in the breeze, and as the higher branches moved in the light wind, sunshine and shade dappled the eyrie making it difficult to determine the correct exposure for photography. The young lay comatose, occasionally yawning. They had bulging crops and looked sleepy and satisfied. It was obvious that a feeding sequence had just finished, so it might be an hour or two before the adults returned. I settled down to wait.

There were many woodland sounds to entertain me. A party of long-tailed tits flitted through the trees, uttering their familiar "tzee, tzee" calls. Parties of pigeons came and went, busy about pigeon business. I could see the remains of the sheep carcase that perhaps had been providing food for the buzzards, and a couple of hoodies were cashing in on this easy food supply. Their antics were amusing. Each would dart quickly in to the corpse, tug for a brief moment, and then hop back hastily, as if fearing that the animal might attack them. A little wren flew repeatedly from tree to rock to top of the hide, scolding these hoodies whose presence she feared.

Suddenly I heard the young buzzards cheep. The hoodies appeared to read this message correctly, too, for they departed swiftly, their protesting cries "kraak, kraak, kraak" echoing back across the glen. The youngsters stared upwards through the greenery, and I heard a buzzard call. Seconds later, the female landed at the nest. She stared momentarily towards the hide, intent and suspicious, then decided there was nothing to alarm her. In her beak she carried a field vole, and dropping it to the floor of the nest, she began to tear it apart. Each of her family were given tiny morsels, and it did not go far. The meal was soon finished, and I wondered what she would do now. The sun was shining brilliantly, and though flickering shadows rippled through the trees, the youngsters found it warm. They sought shelter beneath her out-spread wings, and she settled down quietly to brood them, not moving, her eyes occasionally closing.

After half an hour, she rose, shook herself and took off. I wondered what she was up to, for she did not go off to hunt but landed in another oak only yards away. A small branch covered in delicate newly-opened leaves seemed to have taken her fancy. She grasped it in her beak, and with talons firmly gripping first one branch then another, to give her maximum leverage, she twisted and turned her head this way and that until the obstinate stick came away. Then she carried it to the eyrie to arrange it delicately and to her satisfaction. This proved so totally absorbing an occupation that the urgent calling of her youngsters went unnoticed. Eventually she appeared to be satisfied with her handiwork, and turned her attention to the family.

This time she sat for two hours, a dark brown, sombre bird, so like in colour to the sticks of her nest, that I sometimes had to look twice to make sure she had not slipped quietly away. The only activity that broke her stillness was an occasional shuffling and changing of position, or a ruffling of her feathers as one of the chicks peeped through. Now and again, I heard muffled cheeps from beneath her wings.

Then, all at once, the buzzard hen began to be restless. Suddenly she called loudly, staring intently upwards through the branches. Nothing happened. She called again, more urgently, but again there was no response. Her calls became increasingly impatient and frequent, and at last I heard an answering call from above. A few moments later the cock winged his way through the oaks to land on the nest beside her. But he had brought no food with him, and her cries became really hysterical. She screamed at him, threatening him with menacing beak, and I thought that she was going to attack. He turned away his head submissively, almost apologetically I thought. I would never know to what further lengths she might have gone, for unfortunately it was at this moment that Budge arrived to relieve me.

Two weeks passed before I was able to visit the buzzards again. I arranged with Budge to go very early in the morning, for these are large birds of prey and by now the youngsters would be brought food only once or twice in the day. They would have progressed from small field voles to larger birds such as grouse, and rabbits, and one of these would satisfy their needs for some hours. As we climbed up the hill to the eyrie, the sun was just beginning its daily travel across a deep purple sky. The buzzards were already astir, and we saw them sweep across the hillside calling a warning to the chicks as they flew.

What a change there was! At first the youngsters cowered down, but soon they recovered enough confidence to stand again. We were able to have a good look at them—a comic pair, side by side, solemnly regarding us and not quite sure whether we were friend or foe. Gone was most of their white down, and black and brown feathering had taken its place. One was slightly larger than the other, and appeared to be a hen, for she had an imposing necklace of paler feathers, a mayorial chain of office.

Budge decided to photograph them before leaving me in the hide. The decision was crucial. The young hen chose this moment to turn her back towards us, and I tried by raising my arm and whistling, to attract her attention. She suddenly spread her wings and took off! We watched her glide down the hillside to land on a tree, and knew that she would never again return to the eyrie. Had we frightened her, or had she been about to fly from the nest anyway?

I arranged to have about three hours with the remaining youngster, and Budge had barely disappeared from sight when pre-flight gymnastics were begun. The young cock flapped his wings fast and furiously, bouncing on stiff yellow legs higher and higher, as if on a trampoline. In his eagerness he frequently fell right over, and I wondered how soon he would follow his sister and leave me with no bird to photograph.

At half past seven, the adult female swept in on quiet wings. She had a young grouse for her family, and if she noticed that there was only one of them, she made no sign. It was now no longer necessary to feed them herself, and she departed again immediately, perhaps to perch on a rock nearby, or to resume her hunting. The young male gorged himself, then settled down to sleep off his huge meal. There was no competition now, and he had had a very good meal.

I listened to the early morning woodland sounds. The hoodies were back again at the sheep carcase, and I could hear curlew and lapwing serenading the new day. Oak leaves glistened with summer dew and odd little shivers ran through the foliage as the wind began to freshen. The youngster was soon on his legs again. First he gave himself a thorough preening, paying particular attention this time to the feathers on back and breast. Then he solemnly strutted to the edge of the eyrie, to eject a stream of white waste over the side. Occasionally he appeared to look in the direction of his sister's departing flight, and when gymnastics were once again started with great enthusiasm, I thought he must follow her at any moment.

I realised that this would be my last session with the buzzards for this season, and spent the remaining time planning some of the shots I would hope to get next year. My records for this bird were still incomplete.

93

Harrier Happenings

A young spruce plantation with regimented rows of small trees, regular furrows lined with grass or heather, and deep drains bisecting it at intervals, often presents a rather bleak and dreary picture to the human eye. But to the hen harrier it represents the perfect habitat: ideal conditions for nesting and an abundance of prey. Because the plantation is fenced off from domestic stock, there will be a good crop of grass to encourage voles and other small mammals to take up residence. These form a part of the harrier food supply. Many species of seed-eating and insect-eating birds will also take advantage of this improved habitat, and they will make up a major part of its diet. If the conditions are suitable, larger birds such as grouse and woodcock will be present, and the surplus of all these will also be taken. These perfect conditions, the result in recent years of the ever-increasing acres devoted to the growing of young trees, have been the cause of a major population explosion of the hen harrier.

The harrier is a predatory bird, and there are some people who believe there are too many of them. This can never be true, for unless man interferes, a healthy balance between this predator and its prey is always established. First, the harrier would not be there at all unless there was a good supply of the prey species, and if the numbers of prey fall too low then the numbers of harriers will also diminish. Secondly, this predator performs a useful function in that, of its prey, it will take usually the immature young or the adult that is past its prime, thus ensuring that only the fittest survive to carry on that species.

Another factor that will control the number of harriers is the weather. In a really bad spell during the nesting season it is the young of the predator who will fare worse than those of the prey species, for small birds and small mammals alike will shelter from the rain and not be visible to the searching hawk. The hawk will go hungry, but the small bird will much more easily find the food that it needs. It is interesting to see what happens when such a bad spell occurs, and to trace the consequences through to their ultimate tragedy if the weather does not change.

The day starts wet, and continues wet, and the harrier goes off to hunt. It will quarter its territory meticulously and return after a long period, perhaps with a small pipit weighing one ounce. This will have to be shared between six chicks, and six hungry clamouring youngsters will immediately crowd round it. This is when the first process of elimination will occur. The adult does not choose which chicks it will feed, and the weakest will be excluded from this milling throng. Of those who do reach the vicinity of her beak, only the youngsters who are big enough to reach to its level will receive a portion of food, and one small pipit does not go very far. Only when the bigger and stronger young are satisfied will the weaker get a chance. If prey is very scarce, this could mean death in a very short time, for one day of starvation is enough to kill birds of this size.

If the bad spell of weather is prolonged, the inexorable pattern is continued, the weakest remaining youngster always being excluded from the available food supply. Another factor which may reduce the supply of prey to the chicks is that the adults too must feed, and they have been expending far more energy than usual in hunting. There will come a point when they will first consider their own urgent need, and not the survival of their family. Even in a season of normal weather, it is unusual, where as many as six eggs have been laid, for all the youngsters to be successfully reared.

By the middle of June, Budge and I had come across no fewer than five harrier nests. All were found within an area of 500 acres, mostly young plantation in its early stages, but one pair nested where the spruce was already ten feet high. I had to decide which pair to concentrate on and in the end picked the first that I had found to study. This decision led to the discovery of yet another harrier nest, and a most interesting state of affairs.

I was up on the highest of the forest roads one evening and thinking of anything but hen harriers, short-ears and the rest. Shuna, the labrador, was with me and was having a wonderful time trying to catch up with urgent messages from her nose. It had been a typical highland spring day, hot and sunny, but now the sunshine and heat were fast receding into the west, and fluffy cumulus clouds were building castles on the high hills to the north. It was very quiet and altogether remote from the bustle down by the loch, where the weekend holiday traffic was building up its Friday evening crescendo. We were quite close to the spot where my first harrier nest had been discovered, when Shuna stopped her prowling in and out of the trees, and appeared to be investigating something of great interest. I went to look. A few yards from the road beside a small boulder, and partially screened by the green fronds of new bracken, a curlew had made her nest. In it were four buff-coloured eggs spotted with darker brown, and I decided to wait a little to watch for the hen's return.

We withdrew quietly into a hollow, and Shuna settled down with her customary grunt of resignation—yet another bird-watching session! It was such a nice curlew nest, and so easy of access, that I decided to photograph it. It was only about three hundred yards from the harrier nest, and I wondered how the young would fare once the eggs had hatched. Lost in thought, and planning how to set about the photography, I was suddenly alert. The distinctive food call of a hen harrier broke the silence.

I crouched further into the ditch, and not for the first time regretted Shuna's beautiful golden colouring. A pale grey bird with hawklike beak flew high over the nearby spruce. It was a cock hen harrier. In his talons he held a small bird, and again he sharply called. As he banked to return over the area, I saw how darkly grey his back and wings contrasted with his pale underbody, black wing tips completing the gull-like appearance of the general whole. Though his flight is quite different, you could be pardoned for mistaking him at first for a gull, but you would soon realise that no gull has a beak like a hawk's, nor a tail with brown bars on the oatmeal feathering.

The hen seemed in no hurry to join him, and he circled again into the wind, breaking the silence with another call. Then she rose sharply, a larger bird than he, and dark brown with barred chest and tail. With a preliminary flash and flutter of brown wings in the heather, she strove to become airborne, then swiftly flew towards him with a call as urgent as his own. As he dropped the prey, she neatly caught it in her talons beneath him, then banking steeply returned immediately to her nest.

The cock rested for a moment or two in a grassy clearing on a heather bank. He preened a little, mostly wing feathers, then rose again into the air. Flying low and lazily round little spruces, he continued his leisurely hunting for unwary birds. One wing or the other would suddenly dip, the body totally changing direction in an amazing aerial wriggle as something caught his attention. Then, wings motionless and tail fanned, he would hover on the stiff breeze to weigh up the situation. A sudden pounce by this graceful predator might mean success, and the next meal for his family secured. Eventually he flew out of my sight, and Shuna and I withdrew quietly from the scene.

Hides had now to be erected for this harrier and the curlew. We found both hens reluctant to leave their nests, and stayed only a very short time on each occasion. But both were seen to return quickly after we had left the area, and I anticipated no particular difficulty in getting the shots that we wanted. I was proved wrong on both counts.

I decided to concentrate on the curlew first, and we spent an exasperating week trying to get her to behave. As we approached her nest she would rise quietly, without fuss, and fly off, and we would hear her plaintive wailing cries as she warned her mate of our presence. I would enter the hide, and Budge would make an

97

ostentatious departure from the area. Perhaps some instinct told her there was something alien in the hide, for she would not return. Again and again we tried, but always I had to signal Budge to come and relieve me, in case she deserted.

I was sitting in this hide one day, listening to the two curlew scolding nearby, and hoping that this time the hen would behave. I heard a harrier call, and through a peephole had a grandstand view of a food pass. The two birds met in front of me with the usual calls and the neat passing of prey from one to the other, but this time instead of watching the cock, I kept my eyes on the hen. She circled briefly above, then glided straight down to land just two hundred yards away. I waited for her to rise after her meal was finished, but there was no movement. Could this possibly be another hen and was there yet another nest? How many cocks were there? Cock hen harriers are known to be polygamous, and it was possible that if there were two hens, they were being served by the same cock.

As if to confirm that our luck was in and that we had a very interesting situation to investigate, the curlew now behaved as well as I could ever have hoped for. After some hesitant walking near her nest, she finally decided that all was well. She settled on the eggs, and I took the shots that I wanted. I was anxious now to get out of the hide to discover whether or not we had a second harrier nest so close at hand. I was not expecting Budge for a while yet, so I made little noises to disturb her, hoping that she would fly off naturally and allow me to emerge from the hide unobserved. This turned out to be a thoroughly contrary bird! I shuffled my feet in last season's brittle foliage and I tapped the metal legs of my tripod, but nothing would move her now that she had made up her mind to return to the nest. She seemed to say that since I wished her to sit on her eggs, then there she was, and there she would stay! I would have to postpone investigation until Budge had returned.

When he did, we went straight to the spot where I had seen the harrier land, and there indeed, was a nest with five very small youngsters in it. Three older ones were already clothed in handsome coats of down, but the two younger still looked scrawny and naked, only recently hatched. The hen had risen with the usual angry cries, but now she began to dive-bomb us. Some harriers just disappear when disturbed, but some are extremely aggressive. Both male and female can be very fierce, and sometimes they act together, sometimes separately. This one dived in successive swoops, feet stretched to tear our scalps, all the while screeching her fear and distrust. First the one of us, then the other, felt his hair ruffled, and like a good fighter pilot, she dived with the sun behind her so making it difficult to judge her flight.

I had no wish to alarm her to the point of desertion, although this was very unlikely now that hatching was complete, so after satisfying myself that it was an ideal site for photography, we withdrew. She harried us all the way to the forest road, although her anger appeared to diminish the further we got from her family, and finally she broke off to return to her nest. There had been no sign of a cock, and presumably one or both was away hunting.

We now had two harrier nests and a curlew's, all very close to each other. It was a fascinating situation and one to watch as carefully as possible. We named the first hen harrier, Henrietta, and the second, Harriet, to avoid confusion. A third hide was gradually completed, and each time we returned to the area I was on edge in case the curlew had hatched. Once young curlews are born they remain at the nest only long enough to dry off. Then the parents lead them away to shelter and cover. Once this has happened, it is like looking for the proverbial needle to find them.

We finished just in time. As we were putting the cover over the frame, I noticed that the eggs were chipped, and from beneath the cracked shells came an occasional cheep. I decided to risk going straight into the hide. The hen seemed extremely anxious to return. I erected the tripod, set up the camera, and Budge departed as quickly as possible. The curlew almost threw herself on to the pear-shaped eggs, shuffled a little with wings half lifted, then settled down.

It was two hours, however, before the first little damp head appeared between one of her wings and her body, but within thirty minutes all were born and poking inquisitive little beaks into the strange new world. The sun shone brightly, and what with the heat of the sun and the warmth created by the little bodies of her young beneath her, the curlew panted, holding her beak wide open.

It was a further hour before the first youngster emerged completely from beneath the hen, and it was soon followed by the other three. Legs, curious blue-grey in colour, were cautiously tried out, a stagger or two at first and a sinking down on to elbows for a rest, sometimes an undignified tumble. Short bills were thrust here and there, under this and that. Wings were flapped and hung out to dry off, and a little experimental preening was soon under way. All was unconscious busy preparation for leaving the nest as soon as possible. Judicial-looking black caps of the youngsters were continued as distinctive black markings on backs and wings, and buff-coloured down on breasts merged with the oatmeal and russet of their underbodies. Wonderful camouflage to blend with the stony ground and vegetation of their habitat.

The peace of this charming domestic scene was shattered by the call of a hen harrier cock above. Instinctively the young crowded beneath their parent, who looked up anxiously into the blue sky. She was obviously much worried by the presence of this predator, and twenty minutes later, when all was quiet again, she led them cautiously from the nest into the shelter of the tall grass and heather. This was the last that I saw of them, and I wished them well.

It was now time to turn our attention to Henrietta and Harriet. Harriet's family of five were progressing well, and Henrietta had six healthy youngsters. I was more and more convinced that both hens had the same cock, and if this was so, then he was going to be very busy indeed keeping his two families in food. It would be surprising if all these chicks were successfully reared.

Budge and I decided to take turn and turn about with the two nests, watching whichever one seemed the most interesting at the time. Whoever was acting as assistant would retreat to a hiding place some distance away, and from there observe activity within the whole area.

I visited Harriet's hide first, and I planned to spend this first session in studying the birds. For photographic purposes, I like to find out how they will react to the click of a camera shutter, from which direction they will approach the nest when flying in, and how they will behave after they have arrived. Flight pictures are the most difficult, and for these it is essential to know the pattern of behaviour. One tries for perfect anticipation and an iron nerve that will prevent too early a release of the shutter.

I had anticipated no particular difficulty with my hen harriers either, and once again was proved wrong. Harriet was an extremely nervous bird. I was sitting quietly, waiting for her to return and watching the antics of her young, when all at once they began to cheep. I heard the call of the hen and saw her shadow pass over the nest site, but instead of gliding in to land she rose suddenly, with startled shrieks, to veer away somewhere behind me. The sound of her protest faded into the distance, then round again she came. Once more Harriet glided over the nest, then rose steeply with angry cries. I could not think what was alarming her. She had accepted the hide, and we had watched her landing at the nest many times. Was it the lens of my camera that disturbed her, or did some uncanny instinct tell her there was a human being close at hand?

I glanced at the chicks. Their crops were bulging, and I decided it was safe to wait a little to see if the hen overcame her distrust and fear. The wind rose a little and the youngsters crowded together for warmth. Already a peck order had been established, for the smallest had to be satisfied with leaning against the white down of its brethren, on the outside of the little circle.

Again I heard Harriet call. This time she flew straight at the hide with raucous cries, rising swiftly into the air at the last possible moment. Her wings brushed its heather camouflage, and I thought she must carry some away with her. Round she came to repeat the manoeuvre, and I was really alarmed. If she could not overcome her fear, there was even at this stage a danger of desertion. I began to think of signalling Budge. Then she came again. With angry cries she repeated her dive-bombing, brushing the top of the hide with outstretched wings. But this time, another large bird followed behind. Through my peephole I could see a cock. He remained near the nest site, gliding over it repeatedly. Suddenly, with no fuss at all and just a gentle brushing of his wings against the heather, he landed.

I had never seen a cock hen harrier at the nest before, so watched his behaviour with great interest. For a moment he stared at the youngsters, as if checking that all was well, then re-arranged a stick or two. He was a most beautiful bird, with dove-grey back and wings, and fierce yellow eyes, yellow hawk's beak, and yellow legs in striking contrast. After a moment he quietly took off, and I heard him circling above, all the time uttering a soft crooning noise, whether to encourage his hen or to comfort the chicks, I do not know.

Eventually Harriet found courage to return. She arrived with no food but with some molinia stalks in her beak. These appeared to give her confidence, for after glancing suspiciously at the hide, she arranged them carefully in the nest, then settled down with the chicks. I gave her a good hour before signalling Budge to come for me.

Budge reported that Henrietta had seemed undisturbed by all the fuss. She had received food several times, in a food pass from a cock, then returned quite happily with it to her nest. We waited to watch Harriet safely back with her chicks, and this she accomplished quite soon, so that I hoped she was at last beginning to settle down.

Next day, as we approached Harriet's nest, she flew off in the usual clumsy harrier fashion, her dark wings frantically flapping to become airborne. It is not unusual for chicks to be tumbled from the nest when this occurs. There were two unfortunates on this occasion, and I gently replaced them before going into the hide. All seemed well, and the family growing fast. Budge left immediately, and I sat down to wait.

Alas, yesterday's pattern was repeated, and this is what Budge saw from his hiding place. Harriet continued her frantic flying at the hide. Once or twice she actually landed near the nest, but took off again after a moment or two of angry squawking. Always she flew from one perching place to another, and another, before once again flying in to look at her nest. Once or twice she picked up a beakful of grass, but this time it did not appear to give her the necessary confidence, and still she would not settle with her family.

Eventually, her protesting cries brought the cock to the scene. Once again he had to persuade her on to the nest by flying in

Red deer mothers...feed their young...into the following spring (*Female red deer with calf*)

The forest carries an acceptable number of beasts (*Red deer eating spruce*)

The excitement begins to mount (*Male red deer*)

This is the situation of my Royal Corrie (*Royal corrie*)

The home of a pair of peregrine (*Peregrine*)

A pair of kestrels was nesting (*Kestrels on nest*)

Frieda had had her cubs (*Frieda and cubs*)

The two cubs came fully out (*Fox cubs*)

himself for short visits. But in the end she seemed to be reassured, for she alighted beside her chicks and remained there. All was peace and quiet. By now we had christened the cock, Harry, and Harry now flew to a nearby ridge where he seemed to have a regular perch upon a rock. Here he rested a little before flying off again to hunt. Perhaps Henrietta's needs had now to be satisfied.

Half an hour went by. Harriet appeared to have settled with her family and there was no sign of the cock. Budge turned his binoculars on to Henrietta's site, but could see no action. It was hot and sunny, and it seemed that all the world rested.

Budge was suddenly aroused from lethargy by the food call of a cock harrier. He flew over the ridge, a grey silhouette against the clear sky, and in his foot he carried prey. It was presumably Harry, and again he called, but Harriet made no move. Twice more he called and there was no response. He seemed puzzled by her odd conduct. Perhaps some lingering memory of yesterday's behaviour remained with him, for Harry suddenly flew in to the nest with the prey still in his talons.

I told Budge afterwards that Harriet made a great fuss on his arrival, but he would not leave the food—she must come out and accept it in a proper food pass.

Budge saw Harry rise from the nest with prey still in his foot, and I saw Harriet settle down again with the chicks. But she was restive, and kept glancing upwards. Again Harry flew in with the food, and again he refused to leave it with her. As he rose once more, I pressed the shutter release of my camera. It seemed to trigger off a reaction, for Harriet rose at once. Budge watched her accept the prey in a typical food pass, then fly back to the nest. But she would not stay. It was only a second before she flew again, the prey still in her foot.

Budge told me later that she took it to her heather bank and ate it herself, but I decided she was too nervous a bird to work with. So far as I knew, the youngsters had had no food for some hours, and it was all becoming too risky. I gave Budge a signal, and we quickly demolished the hide, restored the site as near as possible to normal, and removed ourselves to the hiding place as fast as possible to see what would happen. In no time at all this contrary bird flew in with the prey, and remained at the nest. We decided to leave her in peace.

I had, so far, no pictures of Henrietta. Budge reported that she seemed a placid bird not easily upset by movement near her nest, and all the disturbance so close at hand with Harry and Harriet did not appear to have worried her at all. Perhaps she would supply me with the remaining photographs that I needed.

The spell of good weather continued, and next day I went into Henrietta's hide. Her six chicks appeared to be thriving, though the two younger ones were very much smaller than the others. This time I had brought a tape recorder with me, and when the cock flew over uttering his food call, I was able to record both it and Henrietta's answering cry. She returned to the nest and fed her family with none of Harriet's fuss and bother, then settled down to brood them, sheltering them from the hot sun and the flies that buzzed continuously around.

I gave her half an hour, then played back the recording of the cock's call. She paused only a moment before taking off, answering him with her own. Of course, nothing happened. Harry, and I still suspected it was he, was probably nowhere in the vicinity, and soon she was back with no prey in her foot. Henrietta seemed unworried by this curious event, but no matter how many times I replayed the cock's call, she refused to be fooled and could not be moved again.

I began to have the greatest respect for this sensible bird. Then something happened which made me decide to pack up photography of both our hen harriers for the present. About an hour had gone by when I heard the familiar call, "pee-oo, pee-oo". She recognised this genuine call at once, rising immediately to meet the cock. As she did so, the clumsy bird tumbled two of her youngsters out of the nest. One landed very close, the other a yard or two away.

Henrietta was back again within five minutes, and without hesitation, landed at the nest. In her foot was the rumpled remains of a pipit, and she immediately set to to tear it up and feed it to her young. Plaintive cheeps from outside the nest at last drew her attention to the fact that her family was incomplete. She paused a moment in the task of feeding, looked around, then stretched out her head to pick up the nearest of the chicks. This she carefully replaced in the nest. But the other was more of a problem, for she could not reach it.

I waited with interest to see what she would do, and my hand crept to the shutter release. Suddenly she made up her mind. Stepping over the side of the nest without hesitation, she then grasped the chick firmly by the neck in her beak. Seeing the chance of a unique picture, I triggered the shutter, and to my horror the sound seemed to frighten her. For a split second she paused, looking straight into the lens, then took off with the chick in her beak. Frantically I tried to follow her flight from a peephole, but she soon disappeared from sight.

In a very short time, Henrietta was once again back with her family, but she had returned without the chick. I was very puzzled by her behaviour. Animal and bird memories are certainly short, and counting is not reckoned to be one of their attributes. Yet, it seemed unlikely and unnatural that she would forget that she had one of her chicks in her beak. What had happened? Had she landed somewhere, put it down, and forgotten to lift it again? Had she dropped it while flying, and it had been killed? Whatever had occurred, it did not seem to have upset Henrietta, for she continued serenely to feed the remainder of her family.

This minor tragedy, however, made me decide not to risk any further mishaps. We packed up the remaining hide, and stayed only long enough to make sure that both harrier hens appeared to be behaving normally.

During the remainder of the season we paid several more visits to the area, but just to sit and watch. More and more we were convinced that Harry was the only cock, for at no time did either of us see more than one male. When the time approached for the chicks to fly, we made a final visit to each nest. The youngsters were fine and healthy, graduated in size as is normal with asynchronous hatching, but Harriet had only two that we could discover, and Henrietta three. Of the original eleven chicks, only five remained to fly. It would seem that the territory of one cock with two hens and two families to rear, is no larger than that of one pair of birds. Though in this particular instance one chick had been accidentally lost, it would appear that eventually a dwindling food supply will ensure the survival of only the normal number of young for a single pair.

Just for fun we put all the young together in Harriet's nest to have their photographs taken. Much more aggressive now and already filled with the instinct to scatter on the approach of an intruder, the little hawks were much more difficult to handle. Fierce yellow beaks pecked at our hands when we tried to lift them, and strong yellow legs ran quickly for cover whenever we put a chick down. We had no sooner got them all arranged once more, when the largest started the whole process all over again, dashing into the heather with his brethren following after. The littlest one of all seemed to prefer its back to the camera, too, and we were for ever turning it round.

Finally, we restored Henrietta's three to their own nest and made our way from the plantation for the last time. We caught no glimpse of Harry, Henrietta or Harriet. They would be somewhere about, but now the pressures and urgency were all in abeyance until another season's nesting.

Awkward Owls

By the 17th May I was becoming distinctly jittery about the short-eared owls. Were we going to get a pair this year? Both Budge and I had paid several more visits to their plantation, but so far, though we had watched both a cock and a hen hunting many times, we had failed to find their nest. Was it just bad luck? Or had they, for some reason, failed to nest? A helicopter had been spraying the trees earlier on, and perhaps this had disturbed them. But, if there was a nest, the eggs must be very close to hatching. Young short-ears begin to scatter after about ten days, and if we were not careful we would be too late to get photographs of young short-eared owls this year.

Somewhat daunted, but determined to have one more try, we set off very early the next morning, the 18th May. It was still almost dark as we took up our usual position with the car. The blackcock were busy crooning and croodling on their lekking ground to the east, a crescendo of busy voices rising to a demented cacophony as each bird strove to declare its supremacy; a final displaying for this season, perhaps. An early blackbird called a warning of our presence to the bird world, and the curlews, as usual, sounded sad complainings to the new-born day. A pair of carrion tangled briefly with some early morning gulls as they explored the area for food. But, there was no sign of the short-ears.

For half an hour we sat listening to the stirrings of another day. The eastern sky gradually grew lighter, and soon we were able to admire the riot of gorse that clothed parts of the plantation in flaming yellow. It was in startling contrast to the sombre brown of dead heather and the fresh green of new growth on young spruce.

Then we heard the short-eared owl. It called with sharp staccato cries, roughly every five seconds, and with an impatient pleading quality in the sound. It was somewhere on the ground we thought, but we could not see it. A similar sharp call came from above, and we quickly scanned the misty sky for the other bird. Soon we found it, for it was circling the same piece of ground all the time, flying fairly high and sometimes lost to sight in the swirling banks of mist. Round and round it flapped, with slow powerful wing beats and an occasional glance downward. This one was a cock.

With every circle that he made the cock seemed to gain height, becoming more and more difficult to pick up in the grey cloud. It was all a part of the display. Suddenly, he dived swiftly towards the ground, with a spectacular scissoring of the wings and a clapping sound that resembled a minor sonic boom. Plunging earthwards, like a falcon stooping to its prey, it looked as though he must hit the ground. Instead, this short-ear jet plane altered course abruptly, swooping gracefully upwards again with a crazy wriggle of his body and wings. Again and again he went through the performance, and soon we were able to locate the object of these attentions.

The hen was perched on a bank of rocky stones and dead grass, and her eyes followed the cock everywhere as he glided provocatively above. Her cries became increasingly frantic, and she flew to a young spruce nearby to continue her song. Higher and higher her mate spiralled above, answering her call occasionally, enticing her to join him in his flight. At last she could stand it no longer. With a final screech she rose to meet him, and he swooped towards her with another splendid scissoring of his wings. He appeared to miss by inches only as he swerved to avoid her eager flight. They tangled in a flurry of wings and twisting bodies, then off he flapped, not down, nor upwards this time, but straight over their territory. And she flapped along behind.

All at once the hen broke away. With a similar scissoring action to her mate, she dived towards the ground with startling speed, but pulled out of this display flight to glide straight into the spot from which she had been coaxed. Again she began to call, and on this occasion he responded. With no spectacular aerobatics this time, he flew in to where she perched, covered her in a brief mating act, then flew to a heather bank not far away. Much preening was now carried out, both birds carefully attending to wing, body and tail feathers. Occasionally they paused to look around, perhaps just to check that all was well. Then the cock rose once again into the misty sky, spiralling higher and higher until we lost him in the cloud. This action appeared to be the signal for his mate to start her raucous calling again, for soon the air was filled with her cries.

All this action was very encouraging. We had witnessed the mating display of the short-ears, and surely they must be nesting somewhere close to where the hen had perched. We had just decided to have a look, when we were confronted with a fresh problem.

"I think there must be another pair," announced Budge quietly.

Startled, for there had only been one pair last year, I hastily grabbed my binoculars and looked to where he was pointing. Far over in the eastern half of the plantation a short-ear was hunting low over a heather ridge. Our hen was still calling from her perch on the ground, and the cock spiralled above her. What was going on?

We had a hasty consultation. Could there be another pair? Certainly the plantation was large enough to carry two pairs if voles were thick on the ground and feeding plentiful. Certainly, too, the owls we had seen displaying seemed to stick closely to the western half of the area, never infringing eastwards over an unseen barrier. It was just possible that we would have two nests to photograph.

I picked up my binoculars again and was just in time to see, against the pale dawn sky, that our new short-ear carried prey in its foot. Slowly it flapped over the young spruce trees, a straight and purposeful flight, not deviating in any way. "Keep an eye on the other pair," I whispered to Budge, and watched with satisfaction as my bird dropped suddenly to the ground. It was up again in a matter of seconds, but this time the food was in its beak. This was what I was hoping for, for it must be going to deliver that food to its mate. It flew only a few yards before landing on a heather-covered bank, close to a small spruce. Then it took off again. But this time there was prey in neither beak nor foot. It had been handed over.

I sat a moment thinking, and decided that this new development merited immediate investigation. It looked as though there must be two pairs in the plantation and that the new pair was a little ahead of the other in their nesting. Off we went to the eastern part of the plantation.

Able to make use of the car again, we drove as slowly and quietly as possible along the plantation road. For the last two hundred yards or so I was able to switch off the engine, and we rolled gently and silently down a slight incline to a spot from which we should be able to view the new position. There were high gorse bushes on either side, and behind us the ground banked steeply upwards—quite good cover for the car.

It was not long before the cock, for cock it turned out to be, was back again with another offering. Down he dropped to what I thought was the same place, and this time the hen rose from the bank a few yards away to collect the prey. It was a vole, and she wasted no time in returning to her nest with it. She was a beautiful specimen, slightly larger than the cock and paler, but with strong dark marking in her feathering, too.

The cock rose again, and as he flapped his way over the car and away over the gorse to our right, we followed his flight. Suddenly he dipped towards the ground, and our binoculars followed him down. It was then that I pinpointed a small brown shape sitting in the heather beyond the gorse. It was another short-ear! I began to have the worst misgivings.

With rueful thoughts about the number of times the two of us had spent watching the plantation, and how easy it was to misread actions and behaviour, we made our way cautiously over the rough ground towards the nesting position. As we approached, the hen rose abruptly, banked sharply to fly over us squawking fiercely, then landed some thirty yards away. Then she started a distraction display, just as though she was a grouse or a snipe. I had never seen a short-ear do this before. Wings were spread, then one was trailed pathetically as she tried to lead us away from her nest. She turned and twisted, continually altering direction, but always moving away from its position. All the time she uttered harsh, protesting cries.

We found the little scrape nest very quickly. It was partially screened by one of the little spruce trees and two or three heather plants. In it were three little short-ears, of differing size. The smallest one was tiny as yet and had tucked itself snugly away underneath its two brethren. Comical little objects they were, with fierce yellow eyes, and grey hooked beaks that even at this early age were gaping as they chattered a warning at us. Often no sound came, but the gesture had been made in the grand adult fashion. There was still a considerable amount of down in their coats, but dark feathering was fast taking its place, particularly in the two larger ones.

Three young short-ears! In the normal course of events there should be five, six, or more. We turned in the direction of the one that the cock had revealed to us, and moved very carefully. We spread out, walking several yards apart and keeping our eyes glued to the ground. About thirty yards from the nest I found a youngster. He was a little larger than the largest nestling. Forty yards further on another, larger still, was found by Budge. I was pretty sure that the eldest of the family was the one we had seen from the car, and soon we stumbled upon it. It had not moved, in spite of all the disturbance. It regarded us solemnly with brilliant yellow eyes, and offered only a token protest as I moved to pick it up. We stroked its immature feathering, already darkly streaked, then gently laid it back in its heather shelter.

It was just possible that the younger members of this family, who were still in the nest, would allow me to retrieve something of the situation, photographically. We might still get shots of the adults bringing in food. Back to the nest we went to see where it would be possible to put a hide. It had been a forlorn hope. Obeying infallible instinct, the young family had already scattered, and though we rounded them up hopefully, it was of no use. No sooner did we turn away than number one was off into the heather, followed immediately by the other two. We were too late.

III

Feeling more than a little foolish and not a little fed-up, we returned to the car. How had we gone wrong? It seemed, in retrospect, that it had just been bad luck that we had never before seen more than two short-ears in the air at the one time. It was natural, therefore, to assume that there was only one pair. And that pair, over in the western part of the plantation, we had just been watching in a typical mating display. Perhaps they were a little behind the eastern pair, and there was still a chance of getting photographs.

With our tails between our legs, and not much hope, we drove back to the other side. We were able to go straight to the spot from which we had seen the female calling, and two or three feet away we found the nest. There were three youngsters in it, and we were just in time to see one disappearing into the heather nearby. No doubt he was joining one or two others.

Back in the car we watched our western pair once again go through the motions of display, swooping and diving, scissoring and clapping wings, calling to each other with sharp peremptory cries. Perhaps they were considering a second brood!

Seven weeks after this débacle we paid a final visit to the short-ear plantation. It was very early in the morning, still almost dark, and we decided to leave the car and walk up the forest track. We would find a place on a bank where we could lie amidst heather and gorse, at least partially hidden from short-ear eyes.

The sky turned from palest grey to rose, then flamed in all shades of orange and red to greet a fiery sun as it rose above the horizon. We were suddenly conscious of a hovering shape above us, and we gently eased woolly caps and scarves over all but our eyes. Cautiously, inch by inch, we turned our faces upwards.

A young short-eared owl, as yet unaware of human menace, circled above us. He regarded us solemnly, curious about these unaccustomed shapes on the ground. He squawked suddenly, a surprised sound, then continued his circular tour. Soon he was joined by another, and another, and three young owls circumnavigated above, pausing each in its turn to scrutinise the strange objects on the bank. Inquisitive yellow eyes in dark round faces swivelled downwards to regard us curiously. Gradually it seemed to dawn on them that we were alien beings, creatures of possible menace. There was a squawk from one of them, more of alarm than surprise, and then they began to circle higher and higher.

Suddenly there were no more short-ears, and we sat up in time to see the three of them disappearing over the plantation. Off they flew into the mist and the rising sun. Soon they would disperse to find new territories in other young plantations—if they survived the hazards of winter weather, competition from other predators, and men with guns.

Royal Corrie

In the area where I am presently stationed, there is a wild and rocky place, a corrie set in the side of a ridge. The forest below reaches sheltering fingers into its lower parts, and the ridge above offers some protection from cold northerly winds.

The corrie is part, really, of a three hundred foot cliff which stretches for a quarter of a mile across the hillside, and appears as a giant step bridging the gap between glen and ridge. The view from the top is impressive. The ridge behind represents the southern limit of mountain country, and below, stretching south as far as the eye can see, lies a broad, fertile plain. A river flows lazily across it, a giant snake, born in the loch below to meander in a series of sinuous curves to the sea.

The cliff face is patterned with small trees, wherever crevices with soil offer a roothold. Stunted birch and rowan struggle for existence on narrow ledges. Ivy climbs precariously up moisture-laden rock. Heather rakes stretch up and along the cliff, wherever heather can grow. A jumble of house-size rocks, like the grotesque remains of some bygone earthquake, lie scattered along its foot, the result of millions of years of weathering by ice, wind and rain. Black and roughened boulders are streaked with white, where birds have habitual perching places.

This is the situation of my Royal Corrie, and this wild place is the domain of red deer. It is also the home of a pair of peregrine and a pair of raven, who each upon occasion angrily defend their rather constricted territories. A badger family has its sett in a jumble of rugged rocks, and I suspect that a vixen has her den higher up the slope. Here, on a small heather platform within this dark amphitheatre, is enacted yearly the rutting drama of "George", my favourite royal.

George is a splendid animal whose progress I have watched over several years, and I make a point of checking on his well-being from time to time—that is, if I can find him, for he is a hill stag who, as a general rule, is discovered in the Corrie only at rutting time. When I first saw him I judged that he was about three years old, a promising animal with eight points and a nicely-shaped head. Now, he is a proud royal, a thickset massive beast with magnificent antlers. Amongst the dozen or more hinds that he controls, is a beautiful, pale, straw-coloured animal, the leader of them all, and I look for her whenever I am in the vicinity of the Corrie.

In the present day, there are red deer who have their territories and live out their lives entirely on the open hill; there are those whose territories are permanently within the forest; and there are those who use the forest verges for shelter, but who move out on to the hill to feed, or to rut during the season. But, in bygone ages, the red deer used to be entirely a creature of the forest.

In the days of the great Caledonian Forest, when pinewoods covered large areas of the Highlands and fine oaks grew on richer ground in the glens, splendid stags with massive heads, and sleek, sturdy hinds, were to be found roaming the sparsely populated country. They were larger beasts than those we know today. Woodland clearings and pine forest provided good shelter and feeding, and natural predators, wolf and lynx in addition to the fox and eagle, would have killed off the weak and sickly, thus ensuring that only the fittest survived to continue the species. Both these factors would have helped to produce a noble animal.

As the old forests began gradually to disappear, over the centuries the red deer was increasingly deprived of its natural habitat. It was forced to become a creature of the bare hills and glens, and there it survived, but at a price. As a pine, planted at an unnaturally high altitude and in poor soil grows, but is small in size producing only inferior needles, so the red deer on the high hills and barren wastes continued to exist, but as a smaller animal, the stags growing only inferior antlers.

A further deterioration in the size and condition of the red deer occurred in the Victorian era. Stalking became popular, and rich landowners built imposing shooting lodges all over the Highlands. During the season, large parties stalked the deer, the stag with the finest head, a royal if possible, each man's ambition. Many were shot. Only a small number of hinds were killed, however, mostly for the purpose of providing venison for the pot. Thus, an unnatural balance between stags and hinds was created, and each year when the rutting time came round again, there would be more and more hinds to be served by fewer and fewer stags of good quality. Inevitably, poor calves were born, and stock further deteriorated.

Today, we are once again on the upgrade. For commercial reasons usually, but not always, many landowners are now interested in improving the quality of the deer on their estates. In remote or quiet glens during the hard winter months, stags are given extra feeding to supply the necessary protein in their diet, and areas of woodland have often been set aside to provide all-important shelter for the animals. With the planting and spread of large areas of new forest, the red deer is beginning to find its way back into its natural habitat, and the shelter it finds amongst the forest trees should eventually contribute towards a better quality and condition of animal. Already there is a noticeable improvement.

It is my job as a forester to keep an eye on the red deer in the forests within my charge. A balance has to be established so that the forest carries an acceptable number of beasts, and careful control is necessary. Every year, as the stalking season approaches, I have to decide on the number of stags to be culled, and also which animals should be shot and which left to improve the stock. And when the stag shooting is finished, it is the turn of the hinds, and the correct balance of hinds to stags must be achieved. The need constantly to know the situation regarding the red deer in his area provides the forester with excellent opportunities to study and photograph the animal.

After the rut in the autumn, the stags begin to migrate back to their winter quarters, and the hinds, too, have dispersed from the rutting areas. During the greater part of the year stags and hinds remain separate, each in smaller or larger groups; but, as with every rule, there are many exceptions.

Generally speaking, the forest stags will move out on to the hill, but usually some stags will remain in the forest to watch over the hinds that are there. Often a young "staggie" is to be seen in a group of hinds, for he is not yet old enough to hold his own among the stags. Last season's calves will also be found in these groups, for red deer mothers continue to feed their young right through the winter into the following spring. Whatever the size of each group, there is usually a dominant animal, a hind, who leads the group and is always alert for the first signs of danger.

In the summer the males begin to gather together in certain well-defined areas in the forest, seeming to keep almost entirely within these territories, and collecting together in quite large numbers. Then, in September, when the mating urge becomes strong, they move out from these places to establish each his own rutting stance. The forest stags have rutting stances in clearings in the trees; those whose territory is at the verge of the forest on the hill, will take up positions in clearings just above the tree-line; the hill stags have their stances on the hill. There is a great restlessness among these animals as the excitement begins to mount. An occasional roar is heard, and by the end of the month the hills and woods resound with the bellows of rutting stags, as each proclaims his territory and prepares to defend it against all-comers.

The hinds, too, become restless, and soon they are gathered in by the stags to the rutting places. Life becomes one continuous battle as stags compete for females, and defend their harems. Invaders try to steal a hind or two, and the hinds themselves are liable to wander away to feed, and then be led astray by predatory stags.

The fever mounts, antlers clash, roars ring out, battles are fought. It is seldom that blood is drawn or real damage done. It is simply a matter of proving supremacy by the greatest show of strength. The whole business is a massive expenditure of energy, and by the end of the rut the splendid stags have become poor debilitated creatures, battered into exhaustion by this seasonal frenzy. Gradually the tension eases, the roars become less frequent and finally die away altogether. Stags and hinds separate again until the season comes round once more.

Much has been written over the years about the stalking of red deer, and there is no need here to repeat all that has been said. But when you are stalking your quarry to get photographs, and not to shoot it, there is one major difference. You need to get much closer to the animal to get a good photograph. It is a great business squirming your way round rock and through heather, with a heavy camera and various other equipment strapped on your back, or around your person, to avoid a tell-tale hump.

The deer on the hill depend a great deal on sight as well as scent to give them adequate warning of danger, but the forest animal relies more on its hearing. It is interesting to observe how the heads of the latter are constantly raised, ears cocked in whatever direction suspicion prompts. The slightest crackle of twigs from a suspicious source is enough to start them moving.

All deer, whether of the hill or the forest, have incredible scenting powers, and the slightest whiff of your presence is enough to provoke instant departure. And wind on a hill or in the forest can be a fickle will-o-the-wisp, one minute in your favour, the next curling round some rocky promontory or slope of the hill, to give warning to the quarry you are so carefully stalking. In a matter of seconds your beautiful photograph, the one that nobody has ever managed to get before, has vanished forever into the obscurity of the trees, or over the ridge into the next glen.

By the middle of August, the "bird" season is more or less over. All the youngsters have flown and there is little to be seen of the adults, except an occasional bird hunting for food. In this season that I write of, Budge Cavenaugh and I came finally to the end of a hectic period, and my thoughts turned more and more to the red deer. Already I had noticed groups of stags beginning to move into their territories for the rut, and I wondered whether George was

I saw the red flash of his coat (*Male fox*)

All at once she appeared from another hole (*Pair of foxes*)

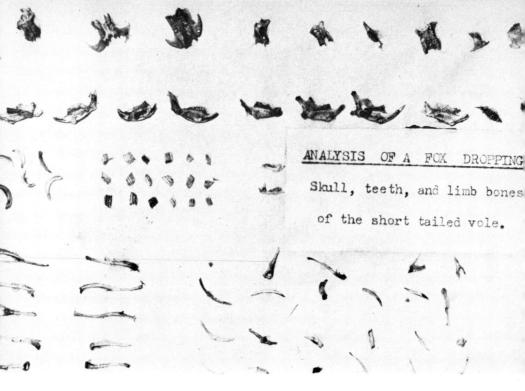

ANALYSIS OF A FOX DROPPING

Skull, teeth, and limb bones

of the short tailed vole.

The findings from each scat were stuck on to a cardboard mount

I weighed each cub as quickly as possible (*Cub on scales*)

already defending his stance in the Royal Corrie. On 7th October I made up my mind to go and see.

The wind had been steadily from the north for a day or two, and the weather pattern did not seem likely to change. This is an excellent wind for stalking deer in the Corrie, for it blows directly from the ridge down towards the forest road, and one's approach to the area is thus always against the breeze, and one's scent being carried away from the questing noses of the deer above.

I decided to spend a night in the forest, and if conditions seemed right in the early morning, to make the attempt on the Corrie. Photographic equipment, binoculars, a sleeping bag and a blanket or two were quickly stowed in the van, and a flask of tea was added to boost morale in the cold watches of the night. By nine o'clock I was driving slowly down the forest road towards the Corrie ridge.

It was a perfect night, with ice-clear sky filled with bright stars that twinkled with a three-dimensional clarity. My headlights picked out a pair of green eyes peering from the dead bracken on roadside banking, a fox out hunting for its hard-to-find prey. Once, three hinds hurried off the road into the nearby spruce, eyes gleaming golden as each glanced briefly at the advancing van.

The place I had in mind to stop lay immediately below the Corrie, on a little used part of the forest road. It was actually the end of the road, and the high banks of the cutting, dotted with birch and alder bush, would ensure that my presence was not very obvious. I slid to a gentle halt, switched off the lights, and sat listening to the noises of the night for a minute or two. The wind, apparently straight from Arctic glaciers, blew a chilly blast in through the window, but whispered mysterious messages in the larch and spruce tops. There was no sound of bird or beast. The forest slept, and so, I thought, would I. It would be necessary to be up well before dawn.

I was not sure what woke me the next morning. It was still very black, and a hasty glance at my watch showed a half after four. Then I heard a mournful bellow from far up on the ridge. A stag already roared defiance at competitors, and conveniently had woken me from surprisingly comfortable slumbers. It was time to be moving.

Something made me hesitate a minute. Then I eased the window beside me gently, inch by inch, until it was open. There was a muffled grunt from the trees close at hand, and I remembered the deer wallow that lay just above me in the spruce. Perhaps a stag was using it. I heard the soft swish of water being disturbed, and then a distinct plop, as if something had been drawn from a pool of mud. It certainly sounded as if an animal was there.

I watched George wallowing once, and it was an awesome sight. There was a place where the forest met the hill and peat banks formed a series of small black puddles. The whole area was boggy, but this was near the centre where the concentration of water was greatest. He had stood a moment shaking his dark head, then turned towards the first peaty pool. He placed first one forefoot, then the other, into the water, then pulled the liquid mud back under his belly and over his sides in a thick black spray. Then he rubbed his head and antlers thoroughly into the peaty sides of the bank beside him. Not entirely satisfied, apparently, he then folded his forelegs and breasted into the dark peaty mixture, pushing his neck deep into the mire, but keeping his nose clear. He rose in a minute, a majestic figure complete with dark brown tidemark along the length of his body, mud still dripping from his antlers and twigs of heather caught up between their points. With a defiant roar he had gone off to do battle.

The animal I listened to on this occasion was not so noisy, but I distinctly heard a body being withdrawn from water, and the crackle of twigs beside the wallow as it seemed to stand a minute. Then I caught the sound of a branch snapping. It came from a short distance up the hill, and there was no sound now in the vicinity of the wallow. Perhaps this boy was on his way up to challenge George.

The thought was intriguing, and I was tempted to set off after him immediately. But, it was better to let him get well up the hill. If he discovered my presence, he would bellow a warning to the world of deer, and not only would he disappear, but I would lose the chance of seeing George as well. I wormed my way into thick clothing, laced up my boots, checked cameras, and restrained my impatience with a cup of tea.

A few minutes later I stepped cautiously from the van and started on the journey up the hill. It was bitterly cold, and the stiff breeze quickly began to find its way through my clothing. I shivered, but was glad, for this wind was right for me and I would have a good chance of stalking up to the Corrie without being detected. I stood a minute within the cover of the trees and listened. There was no sound from the stag who had been wallowing, but I sensed that he was somewhere up above me. There was no sound in the forest except the breeze in the tree tops, but up on the ridge, the mournful bellows of the stags began to increase in volume.

I pressed on again, concentrating entirely upon making as little noise as possible. It was a fairly well worn path from many visits, but in the darkness it would have been easy to miss some new obstruction. I had a tiny torch with covered glass, and this I used to inspect the path ahead from time to time. Suddenly I caught the rank, rutting odour of a stag. I froze to a standstill and sniffed the air, my ears straining in all directions. The scent was faint and I could hear nothing, but it came from directly up the hill, and I decided to wait a little before making the next move.

By now I was almost certain that George was about to be challenged by a forest stag, one whose territory was on the forest verges. Perhaps one day, when George had passed the zenith of his strength and power, this stag would successfully compete for his position. But that time would not be yet, and I looked forward to watching the drama that was about to be enacted.

The scent from the challenging stag died away. I could not pick it up at all, but I did hear a faint crackle of undergrowth away to my left. I hoped it was my animal and moved as quickly as possible to the place I had in mind. This position was at the upper limit of the trees where a spruce, long since blown down in some violent gale, provided a convenient seat just within the forest. From this vantage point I could see the whole of the Corrie, but when it grew light, the trees behind me would provide a convenient backcloth against which it would be difficult to pick me out. I sat down quietly, sniffed the wind again and found it favourable, then hoped it would not be too long before dawn lightened the sky and enabled me to see what was going on.

Nearly half an hour went by. Immediately above me the vegetation in the Corrie, shadowed and dappled grey in the beginnings of dawn, formed a weird sandwich filling between the pale sky and the stygian black of the forest below. A pale, ghostly shape passed on silent wings and disappeared up into the Corrie. I thought it might be a barn owl, but knew of none nesting in this vicinity. The cold northerly wind carried down the deep roars of hill stags on the ridge, and below, deep grunts indicated that forest animals had awoken to the new day and were preparing to defend rutting stances. It was easy to imagine the dramas taking place, and difficult not to catch the excitement in the early morning darkness. I wondered where George's challenger, if indeed he was a challenger, had gone.

Then, quite close, I heard the crackle of trodden branches and the hollow grunts of a stag. It was a sound that reminded me irresistibly of the ptarmigan, not a grunt from the belly, but a croak from the throat. Once again, I caught the rank odour of an animal, and I fretted at the continuing darkness which prevented me from seeing. I held my breath in case he sensed my presence. I began to suspect that this stag had moved just outside the shelter of the trees, and suddenly he roared. The sound reverberated round the walls of the Corrie, and was answered by silence. All noise from the ridge had ceased as, presumably, the stags paused to assess this new challenge. Then he roared again. This time a deeper bellow answered him from the Corrie, and I felt sure it was George.

As the eastern sky began to lighten, I was able to pick out more detail with my binoculars. The cold wind freshened from the icy north and I could see white horses on the loch below. It was difficult to keep the binoculars steady as the cold started really to bite. George continued to roar defiance in my direction, and from his answering bellow I began to have some idea as to where his challenger might be.

Daylight came quickly now, reaching into every nook and cranny of rock, searching out the secrets contained within the Royal Corrie. Daylight revealed George, a splendid silhouette on the edge of the Corrie above. The wind ruffled his thick dark mane and ruffled also the heather of his stance. I marvelled at the spread and thickness of his antlers, plastered thick with the mud of a recent wallowing.

122

George lifted his head and roared again, his neck swelling with the effort. Deep grunts sounded from somewhere in his belly, indicating another volcanic roar about to erupt, but this time, his challenger from somewhere to the left of me, roared his reply first. George trotted forward to stare down the rock-strewn slope. He lifted a forefoot to paw the frozen turf, then shook his head until the matted mane shivered. He stared down towards the forest, and all the time the clamour increased as each stag bellowed defiance.

At last I picked out his adversary. He was indeed about a hundred yards to my left, and standing motionless within the shadow of the trees. Only his head moved slightly, antlers brushing the spruce, a much smaller animal than George, without the power and strength of the royal above. But, he moved to make his challenge.

Slightly hesitantly, the young stag moved out into the open. At once George caught the cautious movement. They stared at each other intently, neither animal making a move. Then the master bellowed again and began to move jerkily down the hill. The young stag stood his ground a minute, but George had the advantage of size and terrain. Not only was he the larger beast, but he came from above down a steep rocky slope. It did not require physical contact to prove the point, and the youngster turned, with a short coughing grunt, to retreat into the safety of the trees, his own domain into which the other would not encroach.

George stood motionless. His thick mane stirred again in the stiff breeze, and I could almost smell the strong odour of his body. Then, from the corner of his eye, he must have caught a movement on the skyline, for with a toss of his head he turned quickly and raced up into the Corrie. I watched the white cloud of his breath as he blew fiercely through moist nostrils, each puff following more closely upon the last as he panted with the effort. He had seen another challenger to his harem.

Then I saw the new stag. As yet, he had not reached the ridge above the Corrie, nor had he spotted George. He was literally following his nose. Head down, and totally absorbed in his hunt for hinds, he sniffed here and there on a well-worn deer track, pausing only occasionally to cast about when he lost the trail. He led

123

me to George's hinds, for through my binoculars, I followed the path ahead of him into the Corrie.

It was comic, really. On a grassy patch dotted with clumps of heather, the sun just beginning to touch their dark flanks, lay fifteen hinds, and all of them completely ignored the antics of their lord, and the noise and confusion around them. Jaws moved rhythmically as they chewed the cud, and ears twitched spasmodically in the early morning breeze. It was a peaceful scene, and strangely in contrast with the restless behaviour of the stags.

As George raced past on his way up to the ridge, only one head was raised. It was the beautiful pale hind that I was hoping to see, and I was glad that she was safe. She seemed to be in excellent condition, and was still evidently the dominant animal in the group. She rose to her feet to gaze steadfastly in the direction of the royal, but soon decided that no danger threatened, and settled down once again with the other hinds.

Meantime, George had warded off the threat from the ridge. But two of his hinds now rose, with their calves of last season, and began to move from the central group as they picked choice vegetation to browse. George was instantly alert. He trotted smartly over, then lowered his head to prod them firmly back into the safety of the harem. Then once again he was watching for the next threat to his supremacy.

George's behaviour was typical of all dominant stags during the rut. He would always be on the move, restlessly ranging backwards and forwards to repel threats from other stags, or to round up straying females. He would seldom eat or sleep, or even rest, and by the end of the season would have been driven to the limits of exhaustion. By then he would be but a shadow of the splendid beast that had begun the rut in September.

I sat and watched them for awhile, and was so engrossed that only the sound of power saws from the forest below made me realise the passage of time. I had obtained no photographs on this occasion, and indeed had forgotten my cameras completely. I cautiously inched my way back into the obscurity of the trees, having no wish to disturb the actors of the drama in the Corrie up above.

Birth In The Corrie

In the spring of the following year, I returned to the Royal Corrie with various jobs in mind. I wanted to find out which eyrie the peregrines were using, and whether they had nested successfully. I hoped, too, that there might be a barn owl in the Corrie. And, as usual, I was going to keep a look-out for George's hinds, so that I could check on their condition and well-being.

The peregrines presented no great problem. They had nested in the Corrie for a good many years, and tended to use one of two eyries in alternate seasons. By the law of averages, I thought I knew which one would be in use this year, and there were two means of access to it. Either I could climb up through the forest and on up into the Corrie, over the boulders and scree, or I could approach from the ridge above and climb down the cliff. It was a glorious day, and I chose the latter for the sake of the sunshine and perfect conditions.

Rowan and birch fringed the Corrie at this point, and it was not until I had squirmed my way out of the tree cover to look into the amphitheatre, that the peregrines saw me. The male had his look-out post on a roughened needle of rock, below to my left, and I could see the feathers of the prey he had brought to it to tear and eat. He flew off with a fierce "kek, kek, kek, kek" of alarm, and I watched fascinated as his curved, tapered wings winnowed the air. Through my binoculars I could see the dark distinctive stripes on his face, and the watchful yellow eyes which never left me. His hysterical shrieks soon brought off his mate from the eyrie, and then I knew that I had been lucky. I had picked the right one for this year, and I set off down to investigate.

This eyrie was a little difficult to approach. One had to make one's way down to a position slightly below it, to a thick growth of blackthorn. From there, one looked up an acutely angled ledge to a little dark alcove, and fresh white droppings streaked on the face below, were obvious signs of occupation. I started, gingerly, to make my way upwards. The rough rock was warm to the touch, the sun still beating from a clear sky into the windless Corrie to reflect its heat from the boulder-strewn sides.

Eventually I reached the alcove, and in the nest were four streaked eggs. They lay on their bed of dried peat, together with soil and pellet remains from previous rearings. The remains of two grouse were there, and once, when the angry parents swept in to attack me, two of their patterned feathers were wafted away from the eyrie, to fall gently to the Corrie floor beneath.

The frantic warning cries from the adult falcons prompted me to remove myself as quickly as possible, and I withdrew to the black-thorn, where it was possible to sit almost completely hidden. The parent birds accepted this partial retreat from their nest. Their behaviour became calmer, and they contented themselves with beating up and down the cliff uttering occasional warning cries. I did not want to run any risk of alarming the female to the point of desertion, but I reckoned it was safe to remain a minute or two to have a look round the Corrie from this excellent vantage point. I was hoping for a glimpse of George's hinds, who might well be some-where around, and also that there might be tell-tale evidence of a barn owl's nest somewhere on the rocky walls.

This wild rocky place may seem an unlikely spot in which to find the nest of a barn owl, but they do, in fact, quite frequently use narrow ledges on cliffs or natural cavities in the rock, both usually protected by a growth of heather or fern. What is more, they will come back year after year to use these nesting sites and successfully rear their families. I know of a nest which has been in use for forty years or more.

I looked carefully round the Corrie for likely places, and on the opposite side to where I was sitting, I noticed a rocky hollow at the bottom of a gully. It was well protected by a luxuriant growth of fern, and looked about the only possible place for the owl.

The female peregrine seemed to have decided that I presented no great threat to her nest, for she had returned to sit. I could see her dark body comfortably settled over her eggs, and now and again her eyes closed briefly. Suddenly, I heard the food call of the male and was just in time to see him materialise from the north, a tiny speck, stooping at incredible speed towards the eyrie. His wings were closed, and in his foot was prey. As he dropped straight towards me, I had a wonderful view of his torpedo-like body, and as he swept up and over the ridge, I heard him call again. There was an answering scream from the eyrie, and his mate took off to spiral up towards him. It seemed as though there must be a head-on collision. But when the crash seemed inevitable, she turned over below him with consummate ease and took the prey from his foot. It looked like a grouse, and she returned immediately to the eyrie to pick and tear at it. Her mate wheeled upwards and away into the blue of the sky, and I lost him as he disappeared over the cliff top with rapidly beating wings.

I was about to leave the blackthorn, when I had my second stroke of luck. A tinkle of rock against rock drew my eyes downwards to the scree slope below. In line astern, a party of twelve hinds, led by a magnificent matriarch, crossed the rocky amphitheatre. The leader was a beautiful pale straw colour, and I was quite sure it was George's hinds I was looking at.

The matriarch led them at a sedate, unworried pace, quite unconscious of my presence, towards a platform of heather at the opposite side. In perfect order, the hinds followed her until all were safely there. Then one by one, forelegs bending first, they gradually eased themselves on to the short heather. Only the straw-coloured hind remained on her feet, and she serenely fed on the first of the year's green shoots. I noticed with satisfaction that already bellies were rounded and pregnant-looking, and that all the animals were beginning to pick up in condition after the rigours of a rather severe winter.

It was time for me to move, though I did so with great reluctance, for it meant that the hinds would see me and leave for the safety of the forest. But it was necessary, if possible, to find that barn owl, and opportunities to come up here during the spring were rather limited, since I do not like to be far from base when there is risk of forest fire, and we were in the middle of the usual dry spring spell.

Back up on the ridge, I made my way to the top of the gully which gave access to the ferny hollow. It turned out to be an easy climb down, for the gully was just a jumble of large boulders, and soon I was amongst the fern. I had just begun to push my way through, when a barn owl rose quietly from a ledge at its furthest end. The ledge was littered with dozens of old pellets, and there was one round white egg. Obviously laying had only just begun. I could hardly believe that I had not discovered the nest before, but the evidence was clear, it had been used many times in past years. I decided it was a possible position for photography and made my way quietly from the area.

I made several brief visits to the Corrie in the early part of June. This was to gradually build a hide for the photography of the barn owl, and also to keep an eye open for any hinds that looked about to give birth. It had always been my ambition to witness this occurrence in the wild, but I knew it would be a stroke of luck not only to arrive at the right moment, but also to be able to get near enough to any beast about to drop her calf.

Compared with that bleak early morning in October when I came up for the rut, the Royal Corrie in June was an enchanting place. The forest below was sombre in hue, but the dark green of spruce was relieved by the delicate feathery branches of yellow-green larch, and deep gullies up the surrounding hills had colour from oak, alder and birch to provide luxuriant contrast. The dull grey rocks in the Corrie itself, were dotted with clumps of bracken, heather and grass, and rowan and birch partially curtained its sides.

The bird world had become increasingly busy. I frequently saw the peregrines angrily seeing-off one of the ravens. Both these birds would now be feeding young. On a cliff to the east of the Corrie, a pair of kestrels was nesting, and further along this cliff, on an inaccessible ledge in a gully, two buzzards had their eyrie. Within the jumble of rocks in the Corrie, a pair of ring ouzels nested. All busily attended to the feeding of voracious families. All was feverish activity and bustle.

I chose an evening during the last week of June to try for my first photographs of the barn owls. By now, the bracken in the Corrie had very nearly reached shoulder height, but though the route to the nest had thus become more difficult, it was now easier to approach it with the minimum of disturbance to the birds.

My hide was a somewhat precarious erection, for the only possible place for it had been against a sloping rock face, on an uncomfortably narrow ledge some fifteen feet from the nest. It was beautifully camouflaged with the same kind of fern that screened the nest itself, and by now the owls had completely accepted its presence. To my surprise, there were only two offspring, and this was a very small clutch for this species of bird. Consequently, these two were very well-fed youngsters and very well-grown. Every time I had come to check on their progress, they frantically clicked angry over-sized bills at me, an entirely automatic response to my presence.

It is a simple matter to check on the well-being of a family of owls during the daytime, but if you are trying for pictures of a feeding sequence, it does, of course, have to be done in the late evening and during the night. In June, when nights are very short, there will be ample opportunity, for the adult birds have a hectic time, not only keeping their youngsters satisfied, but also attending to their own needs.

Since most of the photography must be done in darkness, one has to decide, while it is still light, what particular action one wants to catch, and where it is likely to take place. Many visits, just to watch and decide on the usual pattern of behaviour, are necessary to establish these facts. Then, on the chosen occasion, focussing on the spot you are gambling on being the right one, will have to be done before the light fails. After that, it is in the lap of the gods and superhuman listening powers to gain a second or two of warning of impending action.

It was about nine o'clock in the evening when I eased myself into the hide. Budge Cavenaugh had come up with me to see me in, and first we examined the nest. The young owls had retreated to the furthest end of their ledge, uttering an occasional protest, but docile enough and not really worried by our presence. I suspect that they had become accustomed to my visits. I moved them gently so that they were in the centre of the ledge, then blocked off the further end with a few stones. It then remained to tie back, as naturally as possible, the fronds of fern, so that an uninterrupted view of the nest was obtained. I checked that all was well from inside the hide, then Budge withdrew, and I settled down to complete my preparations.

First, I set up my electronic flashes. I like to use two, for by so doing, you avoid shadows being cast. They represent one of the hazards of the night, however, for when you arrive they are fully charged, but over-use during the night will see you out of power before you have obtained all the pictures you want. This is another reason for those straining ears and the need to perfectly interpret the sounds they pick up.

I focussed carefully on the spot where I hoped an adult bird would arrive with prey. Then checked again that I was correct, and then once again, because the tension had begun to mount and I wanted to be absolutely certain. Then I sat back to enjoy the evening sounds, for it would be a little while yet before I could expect any action. I heard one of the peregrines call to its mate, and knew that they would now settle down for the night. A dog fox barked somewhere below in the scree, warning his mate of his arrival with food. It looked as though my guess, that a vixen had a den somewhere in the vicinity, was correct.

At ten, the young owls began to be very restless. First one, then the other, began to hiss and finally the sound became continuous. They shuffled around so much that I was afraid one might tumble overboard, down the rock. It suddenly seemed to become much darker, night was moving in swiftly. For me the tension became almost intolerable, and I wished it would all get started. In a sense it was easier to relax once one was really at work.

All at once the hissing redoubled in volume, and I caught the excitement of the youngsters. I checked that both flash-gun lights glowed orange, and eased my finger over the cable release to catch the all-important moment. A white shape swept in silently from behind me, but suddenly swung away, to land somewhere in the darkness above. My ears strained in that direction. Was it still there, or had it flown right away? A sharp call came from somewhere close in the shadows of the night. The young answered with renewed hissing, and once again my finger was ready. Once again the white shape flew in on silent wings, but veered away into the darkness.

It seemed to me that something about the hide, or the altered arrangement of the nest, must be alarming it. There was nothing I could do about the youngsters on the ledge, but I wondered whether the lens of my camera might be too obvious. I gently closed up a part of the opening in the hide, and hoped for the best.

Ten minutes later, after an interchange of sharp screams between the adults, who were evidently worried that they had been unable to deliver food to their young, one of them flew in, dropped prey, and took off immediately. I reacted much too slowly and got no picture. But it was the beginning of their acceptance of my presence, as evidenced by the camera and the flash. From then on until two thirty, they came in no less than ten times.

Ten beautiful occasions on which I was able to catch a variety of different permutations of the same feeding sequence! At three thirty, I crawled from the hide—no need on this semi-dark occasion to be relieved by Budge—well-pleased with the night's work and full of eager anticipation of the pictures I should have obtained. Unbelievably, not one of the shots was of any use at all! Somehow the lens had been moved out of focus, and not one of the pictures was sharp.

Of all this I was blissfully unaware, as I inched my way back across the Corrie in the early dawn light. Indeed, I was thinking that as yet I had seen no new red deer calves, and for some time

131

had caught no glimpse of the pale hind and George's females.

The need to try again for barn owl photographs gave me another opportunity of looking out for the hinds. On a fine evening, during the last week in June, I set off for the Royal Corrie to make sure this time, I hoped, of some good action pictures of the owls. The youngsters were now quite large, and put up a brave show of clicking and snapping beaks, as we once more carefully arranged their ledge. Yellow eyes glinted fiercely, and strong talons opened and closed, ready to grip an unwary finger should it come their way. Budge departed, and this time I made very sure that everything was in order, and particularly that the camera was as well hidden as possible.

Night fell, and as if an alarm went off, the hissing of the youngsters commenced. Within a quarter of an hour, the first scream from one of the adults reverberated round the walls of the Corrie, and within seconds, the first visit of the night was paid. The flash from my camera revealed a youngster with a vole in its beak, and an adult in the process of taking off again from the ledge. There was no hesitation this time, and during twelve further visits in the night, I had ample opportunity to get pictures and to study the birds.

By three o'clock, I felt I had had enough. It was a wonderful night, though by now the eastern sky had the pale light of approaching dawn. My thoughts wandered again to the hinds, and I decided to find a sheltered spot near the edge of the forest, where an hour or two's sleep would not go amiss, and from where, in the present wind conditions anyway, I would stand a good chance of seeing animals when it got lighter.

I found a good position just within the trees, and quite close to the place from which I had witnessed George's antics during the rut. The fallen spruce needles of many seasons, drawn into a deeper pile, provided a very comfortable bed, and in the warm June night I needed no extra covering. It could have been only a matter of moments before I drifted into sleep.

Years of watching wild animals and birds, both during the night and the day time, seem to have built into me a sort of convenient alarm clock that rings in my head whenever anything special is about to happen. Of course I do not know the number of times it may have let me down, but I have no grumbles about the luck which has awakened me on many occasions just in time. This early morning, about two hours later, I found myself wide awake and instantly aware that something was about to happen.

I raised my head cautiously and noted that the sun was beginning to creep into the Corrie, and then I saw the hinds. They were away to my right, just on the verge of the forest, and at first I could only see three. A much-trodden deer path runs right along the edge of the forest, and it is joined at various points by those from within it. I was afraid that these animals would come too far along this path, and get too close to me. They were in no hurry, stopping every few seconds to nibble at the vegetation on the hill. Suddenly I realised that the party was bigger. Two more hinds emerged from the trees, and these two had calves. Then, when I thought that there were no more to come, a pale straw-coloured hind came slowly from the dark spruce. Surely this was George's beautiful hind, the matriarch of all his harem! A thrill of excitement surged through me as I realised that she still had to calve, and that she seemed very languid and slow in her movements.

The hinds branched away from the forest, following another well-worn path towards the Corrie. Now the mist was rapidly being chased from its rocky fastness by a sun which promised early warmth, and all the wildlife within its sheltering walls stirred to a fresh day's living. The hinds moved steadily, not stopping to feed, and I thought their objective might be the fertile platform where George had his rutting stance, and where during the autumn I had watched him guarding his harem.

The young calves, only a few days old, stopped every now and then to look around, then trotted fast to catch their mothers. Eager heads were thrust beneath their parents' bellies to snatch a quick drink, but the hinds had more important matters on their minds. Impatiently they turned away, shrugging off their importunate offspring, to press on up the hill.

I watched the pale hind. She lagged behind the others, stopping every now and again to look up into the Corrie, or at her sisters who did not wait for her. Suddenly there was final confirmation

133

of an approaching birth, the "breaking of the waters" around her unborn calf. She seemed exhausted, and I thought she would lie down there and then. But no, it appeared that she had a place in mind which must be reached if possible. Slowly she climbed after the others, who by now had reached the green platform in the Corrie, and were contentedly feeding on the heather and short grass. Then, with a groan that I could clearly hear from my hiding place at the edge of the forest, she reached her goal.

She sank down close to the rest of the hinds, and in a matter of moments her contractions became severe. The great muscles laboured hard as the rhythm quickened, and then, with a final straining, her calf was delivered. She ignored it completely, as it lay in its wet sheath beside her. For a minute, panting a little with her effort, her sides still heaving, she rested.

Only a minute or two passed before the hind stirred. She did not rise, but turned her head towards her offspring. Gradually her rough tongue revealed the brilliant coat of her calf, and soon it began to gleam in the strong June sunshine. Soon the pale spots on its back and sides were clearly visible. She paused a moment in her task, in order to expel the afterbirth, then ate a little of it. The cleaning-up process was soon completed, and the calf tottered to its shaky legs, a little uncertain of itself and the strange new world into which it had just arrived.

The pale hind rose from the ground to watch it. On very unsafe legs, it lurched a few steps in the direction of the other animals, but quickly realised they were not what it wanted. It turned, and nearly fell with this manoeuvre, but made it safely back to mother. She greeted her calf with reassuring licks along its dappled flank, then stood for it as it searched for her life-giving udder.

One minute, by my watch, satisfied its first hunger, and soon it settled down again on the short springy turf. The hind gave it a final going over with her tongue, then apparently satisfied that all was well for the moment, sank down beside it to rest. Her eyes closed, and all was peaceful in the Royal Corrie.

Fox Trails

Five fox bodies lay in a row upon the cold April hillside. They were neatly arranged, with sharp foxy muzzles pointing northwards and thick red brushes stretching meticulously south. A group of roughly clothed men sat around munching sandwiches and smoking pipes over steaming cups of tea. A young lad was there, too, and he sat quietly listening to the talk, his eyes never leaving the bodies on the ground.

One member of the party was missing, and soon he could be heard making his way back through the trees. He looked at the row of dead animals with satisfaction, then lifting his gun to his shoulder, emptied both barrels into the first of the bodies. "You bloody bastard," he shouted. There was real hate on his face, and obvious pleasure that so many of his enemies had been laid low.

This scene stayed in my mind, for I was the youth in the party, and it proved to be a turning point in my life. I had been sick with shame that a human being could behave in this manner to an animal already dead, and was curious to know what misdeeds could have prompted such overwhelming hatred. In my boyhood, the only man I ever heard speak support for the fox was my father, and I do not know whether it was that he had some inkling that all was not as black as it was painted, or whether he just hated to kill unnecessarily. Anyway, very early on in my life I decided to make an attempt to study the animal, and to try and sort out some of the myths and half truths that had become tradition.

It is extremely difficult to see a fox, and during all the years that I have been interested in the animal, few and far between are the occasions I have come across it in the wild. They occurred entirely fortuitously, and perhaps for that reason have remained vividly in my mind. There are many people who seem to be very knowledgeable about the fox, and have an endless repertoire of its sins and misdoings, but when you try to pin them down, you find that the proof they offer is seldom convincing. So that I might have some reliable facts on which to base a study of the animal, I decided to try and obtain a pair to rear in captivity. I would also try, when cubbing time approached, to find a wild pair in the vicinity to watch.

A fox hunter, for some reason, had not killed the last cub in a litter he was destroying, and he gave it to a young man who was a forestry worker. This young man became devoted to the cub, brushing it daily until its coat shone, taking it to work every day so that it became very used to human beings, and encouraging the village children to play freely with it. But the young man had to move to another area and was anxious to find a good home for his pet. This was how I obtained my male, and I was delighted to have this chance of acquiring an animal that should be very easy to handle. For obvious reasons, he was christened "Rufus", and Rufus was destined to become quite famous. He had two books written about him, appeared on television, and even attended a luncheon given by *The Yorkshire Post*. But that is another story.

Next thing was to find a mate for him, and when a friend was asked by an animal society to look for a suitable home for a vixen that had come into their hands, I jumped at the opportunity. This was how "Frieda" came to join Rufus, and how I obtained my pair so easily. I built as large a run for them as was possible. It included trees and bushes, and an area of large boulders amongst which I hoped, one day, Frieda might make a den for her cubs. Here they were able to live as natural a life as was possible in captivity, and particularly important, perhaps, they were always able to find natural cover from human eyes, and to keep well apart from each other if they wished.

Rufus and Frieda met in the first spring following their own births, and this meant that because foxes mate in the winter, they could not produce cubs until the season after the one in which I had acquired them. This gave me an excellent opportunity of getting to know them both before the complications of family life set in.

The young foxes varied greatly in temperament. Because of his early upbringing, Rufus was the complete extrovert. Friendly with everyone, he allowed himself to be handled by anyone, even strangers. He was a bit of an exhibitionist, and really enjoyed showing off. Children he adored, and great were the rough and tumbles he had with them. They were allowed to pull his brush and wrestle with him on the ground. I had a standing bet that he would never bite in earnest, and I never had to pay out. He played with the local dogs, including one fox terrier, and Shuna the labrador he teased unmercifully, for she was far too slow to parry his lightening attacks.

There was one exception to his general good nature, and in this I never knew him change. Some uncanny instinct always told him if the man to whom he was being introduced, had ever killed. I tried him out with various people, those with good records as far as he was concerned, and those with bad. I could never fault him. All his innate wariness would come to the fore, and no reassuring sounds or gestures could overcome his aversion.

Because of his involvement with human beings, Rufus tended to become an animal of the daytime, but Frieda would only come out of her den during the late evening, as she would in the wild. She was a dainty little fox, and friendly enough with those she knew, but very wary of strangers. She was much smaller than Rufus and lighter in colouring, so there was never any difficulty in telling the two apart.

During their first moult, that summer, both looked very moth-eaten indeed, and without their splendid thick winter coats, one saw just how small these animals really are. By the end of September, however, they had grown their new coats, dense and close-textured, a rich rufus in colour and with the sheen of good health upon them. From the first I had been determined to feed them as natural a diet as possible, mainly rabbit and hare. This was thrown to them ungutted, for it is from the gut of herbivorous animals that the captive animal can balance its diet. In the wild, foxes do not live entirely upon flesh, but will take fruit and berries as well. When the need arises, they also eat worms, beetles and slugs. In this they resemble badgers, though with badgers flesh forms but a small part of the diet.

I am afraid that Rufus and Frieda also learned to like unnatural foods, for the local children loved to feed them sweets and other goodies. A particular favourite of Rufus was a concoction known as a snowball, which consisted mainly of coconut, cream and chocolate. This predilection was to prove very useful one day in the future.

I had agreed to let Rufus appear in a film. During one sequence, in the making of it, he was required to pick up a dead blackbird. Now, I had noticed that neither of my foxes liked anything that was black in colour. The object, whatever it might be, seemed to inspire the greatest caution and usually they would leave it severely alone. The same thing occurred now, and nothing would persuade Rufus to pick up that bird. At the end of a two hour session everyone was becoming a little desperate. Suddenly I remembered the snowball. It was worth trying. A number were obtained, and one was stuffed inside the blackbird whilst Rufus was carefully shown what was happening. It was a good thing the cameraman had his wits about him, for the bird had barely been put on the ground before the fox was upon it, and the job was done.

While observing the behaviour of Rufus and Frieda at home, I continued, too, to study the animal in the wild, picking up what clues I could. It is an extremely difficult beast to get close to, being very wary of all human beings, and most sightings of it tend to be accidental. Like most animals, however, it uses regular trails about its territory, and these well-marked paths are easily identified by the finding of droppings. It is necessary to be sure that they are fox droppings, for badgers often follow the same paths. Badger droppings are deposited in a scrape made by the animal and are usually soft in consistency and violet in colour, whereas those of the fox are more like a dog's, but have a distinct point at one end and are deposited usually on a tussock of grass.

A collection of fox droppings would help me to discover more about the diet of the animal in the wild. I chose a trail in the forest that was regularly used, and each month, for a year, I collected the scats for analysis. They were soaked in water first, and then the remains were separated out. The findings from each scat were stuck on to cardboard mounts and dated. This did not, of course, give a strictly accurate record of the food intake, but it did give a rough idea of at least some of the diet. Many hours were spent trying to identify bones and feathers, and after some practice it was possible to have a reasonable idea of what was being eaten. Remains of the common field vole were found in most of the scats, and these were easily identified, particularly during the winter months. Sheep wool, too, was common, and as there were many dead sheep left lying on the neighbouring hills, this was not surprising.

At this time also I decided to try and discover, and map, all the dens in my area, so that when the spring came it might be possible to decide which was being used.

On the domestic scene, 19th February became an important day to note in my diary. As usual, I had gone down to visit the foxes during the evening, and this time, most unusually, I found them lying together. They were on the top of their den, and neither moved as I approached. They were very close together, and it took only a moment or two to realise that they were in the act of mating. Just as with dogs when they mate, the two foxes were coupled and could not move. It had often been suspected that the fox, who is of course related to the dog, mates in the same manner, but so far as I knew this was the first time that it had been conclusively proved.

It now seemed pretty certain that Frieda would cub sometime in April, and I waited impatiently for the day. During the following weeks, Rufus's behaviour did not change; friendly as ever, he was always pleased to see me whenever I went to the enclosure. But Frieda seemed to spend more and more time underground, only appearing at feeding time each evening. A curious facet of her behaviour, though, was that as her pregnancy advanced so did her friendliness increase, and though her appearances were infrequent, she became very tame and docile.

Though I knew her to be pregnant, the signs were not obvious, for her figure became only a little rounder and her body a little heavier. But, during the first week in April, the hair around her nipples began to disappear, leaving a bare area, and I knew that her time was near. Both she and Rufus spent long periods digging holes, which I, as assiduously, blocked up again, for I wanted her to cub in an artificial den amongst the boulders, which would give me easy access to the cubs. Foxes have a quite fantastic digging ability, and can produce a deep hole in only a couple of nights. Their claws are very long and sharp and much more efficient than those of a dog.

From the fiftieth day of her pregnancy, Frieda seemed to retire permanently into her den. Only extreme hunger brought her out, and that would be sometime during the late evening or night. She had become very wild, and if I approached too close to the den, there would be warning "coughs". Rufus, too, received short shrift, and he was allowed nowhere near the entrance. I left her severely alone, fearing that if she was frightened she might harm her cubs when they were born.

On the fifty-third day, I lifted the cover of the den and looked down. Frieda had had her cubs. She lay quietly, with five minute, black, sausage-shaped young clinging to her nipples. A muffled squeak came from somewhere in the busy group, and she eased her body to give them more room. The five mewed quietly, their only concern to grip her engorged nipples, whilst their paws kneaded busily all the time at her soft belly.

Frieda coughed a warning at me, but my voice seemed to calm her. I wondered if I might risk handling her family, and carefully lowered a tentative hand. Immediately her lip was drawn back in a snarl, and as my hand came closer, she suddenly seized it in her mouth. I thought she would bite hard, but all that happened was that she held on firmly. The best thing seemed to be to make no effort to release myself, but to continue the downward movement of my hand. Soon it was resting on one of the cubs. To my surprise she immediately let go, and I was able to gently stroke the little creature. The coat was a dark chocolate in colour, and there were touches of tan on its rather flat face. The short dark tail already had a white tip, and its eyes were shut.

I gently loosed it and picked it up. This was too much for Frieda, who rose immediately, roughly shaking off the other clinging cubs. She gripped me by the calf, and her fangs penetrated. I pushed her away, but she quickly returned, uttering short sharp coughs of warning. Once again she seized my leg. I placed the cub gently on the ground beside her, and immediately she loosed her hold. She picked it up in her mouth, and I had a bad moment wondering if she was going to swallow it. But it turned out that her only concern was to find a safe place to hide it. She ran over to a small hole and deposited it there, then returned to the den for the others.

These were classic signs, and had I remained, the whole family would have been transferred. I quickly replaced the roof of the den, then retrieved the missing cub. Frieda was left in peace to attend to her maternal duties.

There was, however, one task that had to be performed on the first day of life for the cubs. They must be weighed. Later that day I returned with the kitchen scales. Once again I lifted the roof of the den, and Frieda coughed her alarm at me. Again she calmed when I spoke to her, and I lowered my hand gently to fondle her head. Since she made no attempt to bite, I lifted one of her cubs and placed it on the scale. Frieda's confidence had obviously returned, but it was easy to see that her faith in me was under great strain. I weighed each cub as quickly as possible, and returned it immediately to her moist nipples, then removed myself quietly from the scene. This was a job that would have to be done once a week, at least until they were weaned, and I hoped she would gradually get used to the event.

During this same eventful week I examined from a distance, through binoculars, the den where I hoped a wild vixen would cub. It was situated at the head of a narrow glen the sides of which were thickly covered in trees, and could be overlooked from a rocky bluff higher up the hillside, in a small clearing. This would mean a fairly easy approach to the area so long as the wind was in the right direction, and a good viewpoint from above where my presence would not be so easily detected. The den was under an enormous, flat, heather-covered boulder, and it was difficult to determine, from a distance, whether it was occupied or not.

I decided to get a little nearer, but great caution would be necessary, for if the den was in use and the vixen sensed my presence, she would immediately move her family elsewhere. I reached the rocky bluff and had a look. The only clue that the den might be occupied was a pile of dark feathers nearby. By now it was late afternoon, and I made up my mind to wait for a couple of hours. If it was in use, the dog fox could be expected to arrive with food for his vixen, for it is his task to keep her supplied until the cubs are weaned.

The light began to fade as the sun vanished behind the ridge to the west of me. The wind was kind, remaining northerly and light,. but strong enough to take my scent from the area. I heard the fox long before I saw him. From somewhere down among the trees, a a dog called to his vixen that he was bringing food. The usual little shivers of anticipation rippled down my spine, and my eyes ached as I watched for him. Then, suddenly, in a small clearing I saw the red flash of his coat, and in another half minute he was in full sight and close to the den.

There was no sign of the vixen as yet. The dog stood at the entrance, a long-legged hill fox, with prey in his mouth, and head down. He was almost certainly making little noises of encouragement to his vixen, but of course I could only guess at this. All at once she appeared from another hole, which must have been behind the rock. Literally snatching what looked like a hen from him, she turned and disappeared quickly underground.

The dog stood a moment, apparently undecided, then walked over to the dark heap that I had seen from the distance. It was indeed the remains of a bird, a grouse I thought, and he at once began to eat. I wished that I could get closer to get a proper look at him, but it was too risky. Completely unsuspicious of my presence, he finished eating. Then, leaping on to the top of the heather-covered den rock, he curled himself into a compact little ball, brush across face like a large red cat. I crept quietly away, determined next time to get even closer.

The following few weeks at home were fascinating. Frieda was a devoted mother, and her cubs developed fast. Sixteen days after their birth a touch of bright blue could just be seen through slits in their eyes, and two days later the eyes of the two males were wide open. The colour, a brilliant blue, was quite startling. They blinked in the bright sunlight and were forced to turn their heads away. I picked up the larger one, and for the first time he saw a human being clearly. His stare was quite enigmatic and unblinking, but when I lifted a finger a few inches from his nose, he opened his small jaws with lightening rapidity to snap. I put him down hurriedly.

At the end of the third week all were crawling about the den, some more venturesome than others. Whenever the roof was lifted they immediately crawled into the furthest corners of the den, and when they were lifted for weighing, they spat and snapped in earnest. Their teeth were sharp as needles and poor Frieda was already suffering from sore patches around her nipples. Thin squeaks could now be plainly heard from outside the den as they fought over her and pawed at her hairless belly.

Frieda's intake of food had risen sharply, and it was Rufus's job to keep her supplied. Until the cubs were weaned at about five weeks, the food he brought was entirely for her. He carried it to the mouth of the den, then stood there making what can only be described as "wuffling" noises through his nose. This brought her out to snatch the food greedily from him. It was gulped down immediately, and then she went straight back to her cubs. Poor Rufus was treated very ungraciously, and if he made any attempt to enter the den, she flew at him, snarling fiercely.

One evening, towards the middle of May, I went back again to watch the wild den. The wind was blowing straight up the glen towards me and I was careful to make no noise. I crawled to the edge of the rocky bluff and looked down towards the den. It was as well that I had been extra cautious. Outside the entrance was a fox, probably the vixen, and with her were four well-grown cubs. These animals had obviously been born before Frieda's, for they were quite a bit larger. The cubs were tussling over scraps of bone and feather, and I could quite clearly hear their high-pitched, angry squeals. The biggest one had the prize, and the others were trying to take it from him. By keeping it between his forepaws and by turning his back to the others, he was able to hold off their challenge.

The vixen sat on her haunches, apart from the squabbling youngsters, occasionally licking her legs and feet, and only glancing towards her family when the noise became excessive. Suddenly, a jay called a warning from the trees near the den. The cubs stopped in their tracks, then with one accord bolted under the boulder and into the den. The vixen, at once alert, rose to her feet. I followed her gaze and saw the dog fox coming. In his mouth was a rabbit. She trotted to meet him, and he dropped it at once. Then seizing the prey in her jaws, she took it immediately to the entrance of the den.

The cubs were called, and out they came with wagging tails. Once more battle was joined, and if it had been fierce before, it was nothing to what it became now. A great tug-of-war was fought. The rabbit was torn apart, each cub grabbing what it could, then retiring to its own sanctuary to quickly devour its winnings.

The dog now came over to lick the vixen's face, then picking up a crumb of flesh, he presented it to one of the youngsters. The vixen made no attempt to prevent him, which she would have done at an earlier stage. These cubs had evidently now reached an age when the male would take a greater part in their upbringing.

I put down my binoculars regretfully, and quietly crept away. I still had not managed to get any nearer to the den, but I was anxious to do nothing that might ruin my chances of watching this family. It would be almost impossible to find them again, should the vixen take fright and decide to move them all.

One morning early, I went down to the enclosure at home just in time to see two small faces at the entrance to the den. The bright eyes darted inquisitive glances everywhere. Frieda appeared and immediately the two cubs came fully out, stumpy tails wagging furiously, to snatch a piece of meat from her jaws. But it was the bigger of the two who won the prize, and just as I had seen the wild cubs do, so too did this fellow protect his spoils by turning his back on the other. And when the other tried to regain possession by snatching the meat from beneath him, he dropped the food and savaged his brother. I was sure that these were the two males and that the "peck" order had already been established. The bigger cub would get first go at the food. It seemed to me that it was now time to step up their rations, although the intake would still be measured in ounces rather than pounds.

As the days passed Frieda gradually withdrew from attending to her family, and Rufus now took a much more important part in the rearing of the cubs. They were seldom in the den, and the business of catching them for weighing became a very energetic exercise. It also took much longer, and involved many a nip from needle-sharp teeth. At the end of the seventh week I gave up the unequal struggle, but by this time there was sufficient data from which to draw conclusions.

Number of cubs born: 5
Males: 2
Females: 3
Date born: 10th April

	At birth	1st wk	2nd wk	3rd wk	4th wk	5th wk	6th wk	7th wk (weaned)
MALES Average weight in ounces	4	9.5	16.75	24	31	38.5	46	49.5
FEMALES Average weight in ounces	3.4	8.2	14.6	21	27.7	35	40	44.7

Males averaged a 6.5 ounce gain per week, females 5.9.

I had known that vixens were normally smaller than males, it now seemed certain that they were so from birth.

The end of May approached and I thought of the wild family, and wondered how the dog was coping with the increased demands of his growing family. It is after the cubs are weaned that the danger to domestic stock is greatest. Until that time the food intake of a pair of adults is about fifteen to twenty pounds per week, or six to seven good-sized rabbits. The average gain in weight of a cub over the first seven weeks of its life, as has been seen, is about six ounces per week, or roughly one ounce per day. In terms of meat, after weaning, this would be roughly four ounces of meat per day or one and three-quarter pounds per week.

A den of five cubs would need, therefore, eight to ten pounds of meat per week, or in terms of rabbits, three. The normal fox litter is weaned five weeks after birth, that is about the third week in May, assuming early April as the cubbing time. Lambs are often born at the same time as fox cubs, and in five weeks weigh approximately three times as much as a rabbit. Even if cubs were fed entirely on lamb, one lamb would satisfy the cub needs of one family for a week. The danger to lambs from foxes is over, certainly by the beginning of June, so lamb killing occurs over a very short period. The claim that it will take thirty to fifty lambs to rear a family of cubs is therefore ridiculous. It is on dubious claims like these that myths about foxes are built.

At eight weeks Frieda's cubs had stopped looking like puppies and were recognisable as foxes. The facial markings were more distinct, but the coat, which had changed from the chocolate of babyhood through to a smoky grey, still had a soft, juvenile look about it. The tails were thin as yet, but all of them had prominent, white tips. It is not always realised that if an adult fox has a white tip to its tail, it will have had it from birth. The old idea, too, that only vixens have this white tip is complete nonsense.

Frieda had now lost nearly all contact with her family. She spent her time lying in the crotch of a tree where she was safe from their rough attentions. Rufus had taken over their training. He led them around the enclosure obviously teaching them the tricks of the fox trade. They played all kinds of games both with him and amongst themselves, pouncing on odd scraps of food, or, as autumn came in, chasing after the leaves that fluttered from the trees. They no longer kept together as a group, but wandered off into little corners each on his own, exploring a new world as individuals, the first step in the process of breaking up the family unit.

It was now time to make arrangements for their future. Although they had not been tamed, they were in a manner accustomed to man, and I had no wish to turn them loose to take their chance against his hatred. In the end I sent them to a wildlife park, where at least they would be safe from the uncivilised methods used against them by man.

I decided to pay one more visit to my family in the wild. It would be interesting to compare them with the unruly youngsters at home. As I went through the gate that led to their part of the forest, a strange foreboding came with me. For a little way, the path followed the fence, and I found myself following it almost reluctantly. My eye caught an object, a hundred yards or so further along, which was hanging from the fence. It was a vixen. Tailless and undignified she hung there, head downwards, ears pricked forward still, as though she knew her refuge was in the ground. Somehow I knew without any doubt that it must be my vixen, and that her cubs would all have been killed by the terrier sent down to destroy them.

Over the following four years, Frieda was to present me with four consecutive families to study. I was very lucky in having a pair who would breed in captivity, and each year the cubs arrived round about the same time. The size of the family varied from three to five. Each year, Frieda became a little easier to handle until eventually she took my presence in the business of raising the cubs entirely for granted. Every year I kept a record of weights and food intake, and found that the data did not change to any significant degree. I learnt a great deal from my domesticated pair.

It all came to an end as a result of a fearful gale in December 1972. A large tree was blown down, and it fell across the perimeter fence of the fox enclosure. Both animals took this easy route to freedom. Nobody was at home at the time and their escape was not discovered until late evening. I was not too worried, for they had had several minor adventures of this sort before, always returning of their own accord in a fairly short time.

Frieda came in at four o'clock in the morning. She looked rather bedraggled and a little weary, and seemed glad to be home. She would not have wandered far. Of Rufus there was no sign, and there followed a fortnight of terrible anxiety and frantic searching. The gale had brought snow, and the forest was scoured for prints. I found some, but they were some distance from the enclosure and there was no knowing if they belonged to Rufus. I tried the open hill, and found another trail, but even with Shuna's help lost it eventually in a wilderness of rock.

One day, a young man noticed a fox sitting beside the road, a mile or so from my home. It sat there, quite unworried by a human presence, and had the young man stayed a little the fox would probably have approached nearer. But, instead, he went to the nearest house to report. The householder took his gun, and they both went to investigate. Incredibly, the fox was still sitting there and he was almost certainly rather hungry by now. Neither of the men seemed to think it odd that a fox would stay still in the presence of humans, and the man with the gun shot it. So died Rufus, friendly to man to the last, but the victim of his stupidity and hate.

During the winter following his loss, Frieda, for the first time that I could remember, screamed for her mate. The weird blood-curdling shrieks, the mating call of the vixen, resounded round the narrow glen and echoed back again from its tree-covered slopes. I had provided another mate for her, and they had seemed to settle down together, but she would have none of him. The screams continued for nearly three weeks, but there was no answering call to please Frieda.

She lived another two years and eventually died of pneumonia. There were no more cubs, and I shall never know whether she reached the end of the vixen's normal ability to produce, or whether, to the last, she was faithful to her mate.

So ended eight fascinating years.

Epilogue

The greatest threat to our wildlife today is not so much the damage man does directly to a species, but what he does to its habitat. A home is a necessary part of any life cycle, and in the case of birds and animals this is their habitat. So, every hedge uprooted, wood cut down, or swamp drained, means a reduction of living space for some species or other.

Everywhere in the world today habitats are being destroyed by man in his quest for better living standards. He forgets, conveniently, that other living things need to survive too. At the same time he is trying to simplify the complex pattern of nature, to break it down and use it for his own ends. He ignores the fact that the more he simplifies this structure, the greater is the danger that he will destroy it. He tends to forget, also, that he is an intimate part of that structure, a vital strand in the great web of life, and if he destroys the structure, he destroys himself. With his powers of reasoning he holds the well-being of all animate things in his power.

A major habitat where species are safe is an area of woodland. It is the ultimate habitat and must be saved and expanded at all costs. The forest is a complex entity, a mirror of nature, and has the desired structure wherein a balance can be achieved. The people of this country, in whose history there is little of forest background, sometimes think that trees are an intrusion into the familiar scene of smooth bare hillside, or cotton grass bog. They do not understand that the heather or bracken-clad hill and the smooth bog are arrested habitats which, if left to nature, could well become forest once again. A good deal of Highland Scotland is a peat desert with severe erosion problems and a very restricted species structure. Trees provide a blanket to shelter the vulnerable soil, arrest erosion, provide oxygen and give a home to a wide range of species, be it bird, animal, plant or insect. A forest is a complex world, not easily destroyed. Without trees it is an over-simplified world, and one that is very vulnerable.

This is not to say that it should all be left to nature. Nature is often wasteful. But we should work with, and not against her. She always provides more than is necessary, be it blackbirds, fox cubs, or worms, the surplus going to feed other species or to fill vacant niches. Surpluses are an essential facet of nature, and there is no reason at all why man should not use some of these surpluses for his own needs. But it is here that man upsets the balance achieved by other predators. He is quite happy that the robin or thrush take surplus worms, or the swallow butterflies, but if the peregrine falcon dares take a game bird, then he applies a different set of rules. He fails to appreciate that predators cannot help being what they are, and that the predator's prime function is to reduce surpluses and so ensure that only the fittest of the species preyed upon survives to continue it.

All life is predation in some form or other.